The Entrepreneurial Revolution

A Solution for Poverty Eradication

Peter Osalor

CONTENTS PAGE

CHAPTER SEVEN:
BUILDING THE ENTREPRENEURIAL REVOLUTION AND ERADICATING POVERTY: A SECTORAL ANALYSIS

Creating a Culture of Entrepreneurship in Nigeria and

PREFACE

*"If it is going to happen, it is up to you. Accept responsibility for
your life."*
- Anonymous

*"Destiny is not a matter of chance; it is a matter of choice. It is not a
thing to be waited for; it is a thing to be achieved."*
Jeremy Kitson

My Life's Journey and Motivation

I was born into a family of six in the mid-1950's in Warri, Delta State, Nigeria. We lived in a mud house where there was no electricity and it was difficult to access drinkable water. My father was always in and out of menial jobs and at times, it was challenging for us to get a decent meal to eat. From an early age, I began to fend for my family by going to the water side to collect firewood to sell. Unlike us, neighbours and friends did not have to struggle to eat, some took their security to ready available food for granted and their parents would even discipline them or buy them multivitamins when they refused to eat.

I quickly realised that knowledge was key and began to dig deep, as I wanted to satisfy my growing curiosity on the big social differences in society. Why where some living in affluence and others in abject poverty? I had tasted poverty and hated it. It was this hate that fuelled my choice to live a life dedicated to finding out exactly why the world works the way it does.

I went to college as a house boy to a teacher because we could not afford to pay the school fees and that was the best the college could do for me. After college I went to work for Panalpina World Transportation Company in Kano. I bought a house for my mother and established a hotel for her. Then I bought a taxi, started a taxi firm and began to buy more vehicles, however I was not satisfied with my level of knowledge. I wanted more. I wanted to become a global entrepreneur, not merely a local one. I left for Britain in 1983, where I studied accountancy. While there, I took exams to become an accountant and began to apply the knowledge I acquired to various businesses. By 1991 I was a chartered accountant and a chartered tax advisor. As I was investing in my global education in Britain, my wife and I bought two shops in 1995 but had to sell them by 1999 in order to fight bankruptcy. In 2000, we established East London ITEC an IT and accountancy training institute. From 2001-3, I established branches of Peter Osalor and Co. in Port Harcourt, Warri, Yenagoa, and Lagos.

We truly became a multinational global enterprise. Believing I could make a difference of the state of affairs in Nigeria, I ran for governor of Delta state in 2007 but was not elected. Throughout my entire journey, I have gained extensive experience in teaching, accounting, management, capacity and business building. Over time, I began to notice the consistent, predictable patterns and principles that appear to accompany and govern all business and career success. The most important of these principles is having an entrepreneurial attitude. This is what I aim to teach within the pages of this book. It is my desire to guide and mentor you to your path of becoming a successful entrepreneur.

My purpose in life has been the same for more than thirty years. It is to liberate the in-built potentials of individuals by giving them ideas and strategies to fast-track the benefits and rewards they can achieve as successful entrepreneurs. I intend to motivate people by making them realise that success is a choice they have to make and ANYBODY CAN BE SUCCESSFUL if they choose to be.

Putting into practice my vision for entrepreneurial development in Africa, I have established several initiatives:

- *I have established Success in Your Business, a UK registered charity working in partnership with the Federal Government of Nigeria, committed to eradicating poverty by empowering citizens with the right skills and through the development of an entrepreneurial spirit.*

- *I have an on-line TV program*

- *As part of my awareness creation strategy for entrepreneurship, I run a weekly TV program called Success in Your Business on African Independent Television, Abuja. A program formerly aired on Ben TV London, NTA Warri and Port-Harcourt.*

- *I am the CEO of Posag Consulting - a financial consultancy and business advisory service provider with offices in Nigeria, the United States of America and Europe.*

- *I have a business blog site*

- *I am a regular columnist for the Vanguard Newspaper, commenting on the Nigerian economy and policy needs.*

- *I am a founding member of the African and Nigerian Entrepreneurs.com*

- *I am a regular and proactive author in enzinesarticles.com*

Africa's Way Forward

I believe that the present poverty and conflict in Africa as a whole and, specifically, in Nigeria can be significantly reduced by growing the numbers and strengthening the capabilities of local entrepreneurs who pursue the business opportunities available to them. This entrepreneurial development will generate self-employment and grow the labour market, helping to alleviate poverty and social unrest. In order to widen private-sector employment opportunities we must improve the access to rural areas and low income adults and youth to business development resources; improve the abilities of entrepreneurs to manage their businesses and market their goods and services; grow agriculture-based rural businesses pursuing opportunities for value-added processing; and expand government assistance programs for MSMEs. We can do this in the form of public-private initiatives offering business training and support services, including

- Entrepreneurial Training
- Accountancy and IT Training
- Business Start-up and Development
- Agro-Business Development
- Micro-financing and Small Business Loans
- Marketing Support
- Export Promotion Support
- Produce storage facilities development

Benefits of these entrepreneurship initiatives will include:

- Encouraging and supporting women and young entrepreneurs.

- Increased provision of government services to and regulation of the informal business sector.

- Growing rural economic infrastructure and opportunities.

- Grant fund buy-ins from national and international development agencies and NGOs committed to poverty alleviation, youth's empowerment, private sector business development, fair trade, etc.

- Enhancing the quality and competitiveness of Nigerian business.

- Increased capacity to adopt new business technologies.

- Strengthening the organisational and business linkages between the formal and informal sectors.

- Creating and enhancing economic opportunities for school leavers and university and college graduates

This book is written specifically to inspire individuals to start their own businesses and to urge African governments to support entrepreneurial development.

FOREWORD

Peter Osalor has in this book 'The Entrepreneurial Revolution: A solution For Poverty Eradication' boosted the literature and ideas on entrepreneurial studies. The author wrote having in mind the academia, students, political, economic and business managers. He moved the subject matter to global, continental and national dialectics. The reader is carried on from understanding the differences in applied meanings of terms like "entrepreneur" and "entrepreneurism" to historical and economic dynamism of Africa, Nigeria and the place of the entrepreneur and operation, entrepreneurism is securing prosperity and wealth of nations and individuals.

This book is highly recommended for researchers, policy makers, businessmen and women and for teaching and enriching the syllabus of entrepreneurial studies in Africa tertiary institutions. In the Nigerian and African situation the book addressed the challenges of entrepreneurship, poverty alleviation and the way out of the malady. It also addressed specific enterprises such as fishing, livestock, and agriculture broadly defined. Empowerment methodology for various populations cohorts especially women and youth were also handled by the author.

These are general issues and matters addressed to make the book a compel to read and own in every one's and institutional libraries.

Prof Park .O. Idisi
Departments of Agricultural Economics and Extension
Economics, University of Abuja

FOREWORD

The economic turbulence in our world today which has made job securities to be volatile has probably created a ground swell for interest in business ownership and the expression of entrepreneurial skills. In spite of the presence of university education in our world for almost 1000 years, no school offered a degree in entrepreneurship until the 1970s. In the 70s there were only 16 universities that offered courses in entrepreneurship in the whole of the USA, today, over 1,600 do. Prior to that, every course directed people to learn how to manage a business on behalf of others. There are several reasons why the ownership of business is preferable to job seeking or the pursuit of employment.

A business gives you the opportunity to take your future in your own hands. Like they say in Latin Carpe Diem seize the moment. A business quite unlike employment can be inherited by your children, therefore giving you the opportunity to create generational blessings and prosperity for your family. That is why today we see the Ford Motor companies, Heinz, Rolls Royce, which was started by Mr. Rolls and Mr. Royce. The examples are endless.The best that can come out of employment is a salary and a possible pension. Whereas, a business can help you to build equity into the future. At a particular age, the statutory laws of employment of a country make your departure from gainful employment mandatory. While in your own business, you can continue to run in your golden age.

Furthermore, if anything makes the desire to have a business even more likable, it will be the fact that you can make a difference in your world as your company gets involved in corporate social responsibilities through the use of its profit or monies set apart to help meet social needs. You are able to provide employment for others and become part of the solution in your world. We might just rest our argument for business by saying that it helps you to leave a legacy.

However, what is the use having such a desire to run business and yet be poorly informed on how, why and which way to run it.

The author of this book, **Mr. Peter Osalor** takes us into the world of business by introducing to us four books that can set us in motion to start, perpetuate and run a successful business.

- Why and How to start your own business
- How to prepare a business plan
- How to identify and fund your business
- The entrepreneurial revolution – a solution for poverty eradication.

He brings in a fresh insight on the modalities for starting a business that will last. Yes, businesses that will last because 80% of businesses started here in the UK for example fail within 5 years. However, Peter has helped us with the effective steps that can help a successful business. He gives us a step by step guide on how to prepare a business plan and how to run it effectively.

Many businesses also die because they do not know how to leverage by seeking for funds that would make such vision run well. Using his training as a chartered Accountant and Tax specialist, Peter helps us to grasp the possibilities of a successful business as he gives us trade secrets for succeeding in the world of entrepreneurship.

The books of Peter Osalor come highly recommended firstly because of his educated mind. Secondly, because of the practical experience he has had with over 30 years of involvement in business and thirdly as a man who has opened up business in Europe and across Africa. His experience traverses continents and any investment in this works will be more than value for money.

Matthew Ashimolowo
Speaker, Entrepreneur, Philanthropist

ACKNOWLEDGEMENTS

To start with, I would like to thank God for enabling me make this book a reality, to Him alone be all the glory and honour. My profound thanks goes to my family, most especially my wife Mrs. Eudora Osalor who has always given me the support I have needed, every time I need it; your inestimable help is deeply appreciated. My daughter Peace Ani and her husband Chijoke Ani.

My thanks also go to Joseph Akpebu, a key member of my organisation for the relentless effort you have shown towards the production of this book, thank you so much. I would also like to thank Johnson Akpebu for his time and effort.

My sincere thanks also to Dr Abiodun Awomolo and Dr Hashim Gibrill both of Atlanta, USA, for their efforts in critically reviewing and helping put this book together. Mrs Ade D'Almeida for her contribution and inspiration and Pastor Matthew Ashimolowo my spiritual father and pastor, who has been a great source of inspiration in the writing of this book.

My sincere gratitude to Harry Koranteng, "my right hand man" for his time and effort.

To all my staff in London, Port-Harcourt, Warri, Yenagoa, Abuja and to Joseph and Hikmot Ademosu, I say many thanks for your support and commitment; you're all very much appreciated. Limitation of space does not permit me to individually acknowledge the innumerable number of friends and well wishers, thank you so much.

My message to you all is that this is just the beginning; the sky can never be our limit but only our starting point. Let's keep the fire burning.

Thank you

INTRODUCTION

This book concerns the critical role of entrepreneurship in addressing the poverty crisis in Africa and other regions of the developing world. The analysis presented makes clear that if Africa is to escape the current cycle of poverty in which more than half of its billion inhabitants live on less than $2 per day, then it must commit wholeheartedly to pursuing an entrepreneurial revolution. There is no other way.

The Entrepreneurial Revolution argues that governments across Africa must refocus their policy agendas to encourage the start-up and growth of small and medium enterprises (SMEs) that will provide self-employment opportunities, create jobs, and diversify economies. The world's largest economy, the United States, is based on encouraging the passions and talents of entrepreneurs. The world's second largest economy, China, whose population exceeds that of the African continent, has been able to achieve explosive growth and lift millions out of poverty because of an entrepreneurial revolution. India has also done likewise. From Asia to Latin America to Central Europe, governments have come to realise that they must create the environment in terms of infrastructure, legal structures, financial supports, training, and research that will facilitate entrepreneurship. These governments recognise that previous policies have failed to alleviate poverty: large scale government owned enterprises (parastatals) have not done it, privatisation without encouraging individuals to seize opportunities to pursue entrepreneurship has not done it, relying on government handouts and charitable endeavours, no matter how well intentioned, has not done it. Individuals must be empowered to lift themselves and their communities out of a bare subsistence lifestyle, and take their economic destiny into their own hands. This is what an entrepreneurial revolution can achieve. This is not wishful thinking or crass ideological posturing. Asia has been transformed by an entrepreneurial revolution and Africa can be similarly transformed.

16

Such a revolution will build on Africa's human and natural resources to grow and diversify Africa's economy and, thereby, finally address the poverty crisis. This kind of revolution can and will not happen overnight, but it can happen. If governments and individuals do not develop the correct mindset and will to pursue this entrepreneurial revolution then we will fail to see it take place.

Using Nigeria, Africa's most populous nation and third largest economy, as a case study this book discusses entrepreneurship and the entrepreneurial revolution, reviews the history of entrepreneurship in Africa, assesses the challenges and opportunities for the African entrepreneurial revolution, and provides blueprints for governments and encouragement for individuals to pursue the entrepreneurial revolution. *The Entrepreneurial Revolution* provides the vision, and lays out the means whereby vision can become reality. This is not an arcane academic treatise, but rather a call to action. If Africa is to realise its immense potential and do what is fitting for its millions of poverty-stricken citizens, then an ENTREPRENEURIAL REVOLUTION is the surest way – the only away – to achieve such a goal.

CHAPTER ONE

INTRODUCTION:
THE ENTREPRENEURIAL IMPERATIVE

"Some people dream of great accomplishments, while others stay awake and do them."

Anonymous

The core argument of this book is that the present widespread poverty and conflict in Nigeria, and Africa as a whole, can be significantly reduced by growing the numbers and strengthening the capabilities of local entrepreneurs. In order to bring this about an entrepreneurial revolution must be undertaken that encompasses individual entrepreneurship and sharply focused supportive government policies and actions. This entrepreneurial revolution will create self-employment, provide jobs, grow and diversify the economy, and, as a direct result, diminish poverty and it's related economic misery and social unrest. This is a grand argument; its fundamental truth is detailed in the pages that follow.

Definitions and Debates

We will begin by looking at the entrepreneurial revolution and poverty alleviation by addressing the following fundamental questions:

Who is an Entrepreneur? What does he or she do? What are the psychological and social characteristics of entrepreneurs?

What is Entrepreneurship? What activities does it involve? What does it contribute to society?

What is Entrepreneurialism? Is it universal across time and space, from society to society? What social and political factors support or hinder entrepreneurialism? What impact does it have on economic development?

What is an Entrepreneurial Revolution? What are its key features? How can it be achieved? What impacts will it have?
What are the causes and dimensions of poverty in Africa?

Is it an exaggeration to say that anybody can be an entrepreneur? Is having the right attitude all it takes to become an entrepreneur? As a practising entrepreneur, I believe an entrepreneur is someone who uses their creativity to create economic value for the benefit of themselves and society. The word entrepreneur was first applied in France to individuals who "entered" (entre) and took charge (preneur). These individuals were those who took charge of their destiny.

Others define an entrepreneur as:

Someone who assumes the financial risk of the initiation, operation and management of a business (Entrepreneur.com);

A person who habitually creates and innovates to build something of recognised value around perceived opportunities (Kotelnikov)

Those individuals who launch enterprises that commercialise new products, services, or processes that contribute to economic growth. (Baumol)

[those who] Bring the new technologies and the new concepts into active commercial use. They are the change agents of capitalism. (Lester Thurow)

The person who perceives the market opportunity and then has the motivation, drive and ability to mobilise resources to meet it(Di-Masi)

A person who undertakes a wealth-creating and value-adding process, through incubating ideas, assembling resources and making things happen (Tan, quoting Kao)

We can therefore state that an entrepreneur is a person who is driven to establish a business to take advantage of the financial opportunities and personal fulfilment offered, by pursuing their own dreams and shaping their own destiny in local, national, and global economies.

There is broad agreement that characteristically an entrepreneur is:

- Self confident and multi-skilled.

- Confident in the face of difficulties and discouraging circumstances.

- Not an 'inventor' in the traditional sense but one who is able to carve out a new niche in the market place, often invisible to others.

- Results-oriented: To be successful requires the drive that only comes from setting goals and targets and obtaining pleasure from achieving them.

- A risk-taker: To succeed means taking measured risks.

- A risk-assessor: In today's economic climate starting a business can be less risky than conventional employment.

- Totally committed: a person who will do whatever it takes to be successful in business: Hard work, energy and single-mindedness are essential elements in the entrepreneurial profile.

- Visionary and optimistic: In new and emerging businesses, the person who starts the business is often an entrepreneur who believes that with the right resources anything can be achieved.

- A participant, not an observer; a player, not a fan.

- A course-setter: The entrepreneur likes to be in control of his or her future (Di-Masi; Entrepreneur.com)

What do these characteristics mean for Mr. or Mrs. Anybody who wants to be an entrepreneur? It means he or she must have a change of attitude. He or she must go from begging for a job, a contract, a hand out, or food to following their talent to meet the needs of others in order to generate profit. The quintessential, renowned entrepreneur Richard Branson states:

> Entrepreneurship is not about getting one over on the customer. It's not about working on your own. It's not about looking out for number one. It's not necessarily about making a lot of money. It is absolutely not about letting work

take over your life. On the contrary, it's about turning what excites you in life into capital, so that you can do more of it and move forward with it. I think Entrepreneurship is our natural state – a big adult word that probably boils down to something much more obvious like playfulness (Branson).

An entrepreneur must shun the unpatriotic attitude of nepotism, trying to get ahead through family and other connections. If one seeks to provide a good product or service then people will buy it – regardless of ethnicity, age, or gender. You don't have to be an inventor or create a new product to make it in the market; simply have a product you are passionate about and you will find buyers.

As an entrepreneur, you will need to set goals and stick to them. There will be days when everything goes well, and days when you are challenged; regardless of the type of day you are having, you must press on to achieve your goals. You cannot blame anybody for your failure and you cannot afford to neglect your own future. In today's world, there are no jobs been handed out and even if you get a job today, it's likely that it will not be there tomorrow. An entrepreneur is an active participant both in his or her success and also in society's progression. If you take the leap to becoming an entrepreneur, there are copious experiences that await you.

Entrepreneurship

Entrepreneurship is an elusive concept. Analysts note that "defining entrepreneurship is not an easy task. There are almost as many definitions of entrepreneurship as there are scholarly books on the subjects." (FAO) At core, entrepreneurship involves both the actions and outlook of entrepreneurs. Beginning with the earliest known definition in the eighteenth century, entrepreneurship is said to involve risk-taking, bringing together the factors of production, business innovation, and enterprise start-up. (Di-Masi)

Entrepreneurship is also described as "the art of finding creative profitable solutions to problems." (Kotelnikov)

Benefits and Challenges of Entrepreneurship

There are several benefits to taking the risk, becoming an entrepreneur, and opening up your own business venture. There are also a lot of challenges involved in entrepreneurship including the risk factor and the chance of failure, both of which are greatly increased when the surroundings for your business are not ideal, however, the freedom, the financial success and the job security are a few. The benefits outweigh the challenges. Any business person must assess the internal and external factors that may contribute to the success or failure of their business before deciding to go through with the venture. Being an entrepreneur requires a great amount of sales and marketing skill. This may put some people off for the fear of being labelled a 'salesperson'.

Notwithstanding the connotations of this term, there is no business that can progress without an aggressive sales strategy. It is necessary from time to time to conduct frequent reviews of how the business is faring in order to make a progress rating. As entrepreneurship is dynamic, much thought has to be invested in coming up with new innovations to enhance business. Consumers' needs change so often, therefore, new strategies need to be put in place and old methods reviewed regarding their effectiveness.

A recent study, the *Making of a Successful Entrepreneur*, (Wadhwa, et al, 2009) reveals some very interesting, key findings about the motivations, challenges, and mindset of U.S. entrepreneurs.

According to entrepreneurs surveyed:

Core challenges in starting and running a successful business are the time and effort required, capital,financing, and experience in running a business.

Reasons why individuals may not pursue entrepreneurship include lack of willingness or of ability to take risks, and to devote the time and effort; difficulty in raising capital; deficiencies in business management skills, knowledge of how to start a business, and knowledge about the industry and markets; and family or financial pressures to keep a traditional, steady job.

Sources of funding for entrepreneurial endeavours are derived first and foremost from founders' personal savings, this is especially so for first-time businesses; it becomes easier for some entrepreneurs to raise angel and venture funding after they have started more companies. Other factors mentioned, pointing to the mindsets of successful entrepreneurs, are faith and God, hard work, perseverance or determination, timing, spouse forbearance and support, optimism, naivety, and a willingness to risk everything.

Importantly the entrepreneurs highlighted the unanticipated challenges they faced, these being business related stress, maintaining a balance in life, understanding and developing products for constantly changing markets, government regulations taxes and costs of employee benefits, and a lack of knowledge about raising capital.

The study concluded, that given the fact that entrepreneurship makes such a marked contribution to the size and dynamism of the U.S., with small businesses generally creating "60 to 80 percent of the net new employment in the United States"

Understanding what makes entrepreneurs successful could help develop better policies to foster entrepreneurship and increase the numbers of high-growth companies.

Studies on the backgrounds of entrepreneurs also show that many, although by no means all, share common experiences of a growing up in deprived circumstances, membership in minority or marginalised social groups, and a newcomer, immigrant family background. (Di-Masi)

Based on my experience, and from my own entrepreneurial mindset, business owners are divided in to two categories – entrepreneurs and self-employed. For many these may seem as one and the same thing; however they have a distinct difference. An entrepreneur is a business proprietor who carries out business and maintains growth while getting satisfaction from all business activities. The entrepreneurial mindset is that of a strategist and a visionary. On the other hand, a self-employed business person is one who simply seeks to tap a financial niche without much regard for objective, forward-looking planning. This type of business person may not necessarily enjoy what they do. While an entrepreneur is focused on growth and expansion, a self-employed business owner may be content with the current income levels, thus seeing no need for new strategies. Entrepreneurs are good strategists and, therefore, not afraid to take calculated risks after making a careful assessment of the business situation.

The moment an entrepreneurial mindset has been mastered, any type of business, whether big or small, is able to achieve significant growth. Entrepreneurs in most cases have satisfying personal lives because they ensure that all aspects are catered for. It is of no use having a flourishing enterprise at the expense of a fulfilling personal life. Entrepreneurship can aptly be described as a business lifestyle, in contrast to regular business self-employment which is merely an activity. The entrepreneurial mindset is able push business towards greater heights.

We can conclude that entrepreneurs exhibit a *carpe diem* spirit; they are driven to "seize the moment." Often this spirit of enterprise has been shaped by an underprivileged background. Increasingly, entrepreneurs are created by the need to cope with the present global economic downturn. In the larger, developed economies corporate jobs are disappearing as companies downsize or even disappear; in the developing economies the private sector jobs have not been created and the government, public sector jobs are being slashed.

Entrepreneurialism

In order to go about the business of enterprise start-up and growth, entrepreneurs need a supportive, conducive social and political environment. They need governments that encourage and facilitate entrepreneurship; they need an economic system that rewards the risk-taker and innovator; and they also benefit from a culture that respects and champions the entrepreneur.

Entrepreneurialism again has many definitions; it is often used as a synonym for entrepreneurship. However, it is also seen as a co-operative relationship between the government and entrepreneurs, between the public and private sectors. (OECD) In this book we use the term entrepreneurialism to denote a capitalist, free market economy where innovation, job creation, and income growth are driven by the talents and initiatives of entrepreneurs in a supportive relationship with government. This is similar to the notion of Entrepreneurial Capitalism, "which involves innovative and productive entrepreneurs ... those individuals who launch enterprises that commercialise new products, services, or processes that contribute to economic growth." These private sector individuals are supported by public policies that allow "citizens from all walks of life have the opportunity to become innovative entrepreneurs." (Baumol)

Debating Entrepreneurialism – Is It All Good?

Professor Wee-Liang Tan reminds us that the pursuit of the profit motive alone can devalue the worth of entrepreneurialism to society; that it is difficult to serve both "God and mammon." While we champion entrepreneurialism and the contributions entrepreneurs make to the shape and dynamics of our economies, we know that entrepreneurs and entrepreneurialism do not always work for the "common good. Throughout Africa, including notably Nigeria, and across the world we see many examples of duplicitous business men and women and corrupt government officials, who hide self-serving pursuits under the guise of entrepreneurialism. Among the major challenges to Micro, Small, and Medium Enterprises (MSMEs) growth in developing economies is "a high level of corruption." (Kaufmann, et al) Transparency International highlights the high levels of business sector corruption in such emerging and transitional economies as China, India, Brazil, Russia, Indonesia, Mexico, Turkey and Vietnam, (Nawaz) and argues in relation to Africa that:
Despite recent progress in democracy and human rights in a number of African countries, corruption remains one of the biggest challenges throughout the continent. (Transparency International)
Tan advocates that we should adopt the tenets that "an entrepreneurial society is one in which the economic activities are directed at creating wealth and adding value for the individual" and to society and that the "central belief" of entrepreneurialism "is that society should organise its economic activities not solely on the basis of the profit motive, but also on value to society". (Tan)

This is a tall order. Balancing individual reward with contributions to the common good is one of the core challenges of entrepreneurialism.

Entrepreneurialism's Impact on Economic Growth and Development

Analysts' have come to realise that entrepreneurs (those businessmen and women who produce, sell, and innovate) are the backbone of modern economies. Entrepreneurs take risks and open up doors to whole new business worlds. It is their important contributions that help society grow as a whole. One of the reasons the United States is such a dynamic, innovative, and prosperous nation is because of the numerous business entrepreneurs that take their ideas to the next level regardless of the risks involved. Entrepreneurs create jobs and innovate and grow the economy. The creativity and impact of U.S. entrepreneurs was clearly acknowledged in President Obama's 2010 State of the Union address he stated:

> Now, the true engine of job creation in this country will always be America's businesses. But government can create the conditions necessary for businesses to expand and hire more workers. We should start where most new jobs do –- in small businesses, companies that begin when an entrepreneur takes a chance on a dream, or a worker decides it's time she became her own boss. Through sheer grit and determination, these companies have weathered the recession and they're ready to grow. (Obama)

The millions of small and medium-sized firms started by entrepreneurs provide the innovations and create the jobs intrinsic to economic growth and development. Many goods and services we take for granted "were introduced by entrepreneurs -- telephone service, the automobile, the airplane, air conditioning, the personal computer and accompanying software. None of us can know what promising new technologies await us in the future. But if the past is any guide to the future, then one thing is virtually certain: most of them will be developed by entrepreneurs." (Baumol)

According to Schumpeter (1975) capital and output growth in an economy depends significantly on the entrepreneur. The quality of performance of the entrepreneur determines whether capital grows rapidly or slowly, and whether the growth involves innovation where new products and production techniques are developed. The difference in economic growth rates of countries is largely due to the quality of their entrepreneurs. Factors of production, land, labour and capital, will lie dormant or become indolent without the entrepreneur who organises them for productive ventures. The entrepreneur is, therefore, an important agent of growth, innovation and technical progress.

China's explosive economic growth over the past 25 years is due largely to removing ownership, bureaucratic, and financial limits on the entrepreneurial drive of the Chinese people. At the heart of other rapidly growing economies such as India and Brazil are numerous small and medium scale manufacturing, retail, IT, technical, and financial firms. In the United States, the world's biggest and most sophisticated economy, 75% of the 16 million businesses are run as sole proprietorships (Entrepreneur.com) The U.S. Small Business Administration recognises that "small business is critical to our economic recovery and strength, to building America's future, and to helping the United States compete in today's global marketplace." (SBA). In many developing countries, including Nigeria, small and medium enterprises (run according to the visions, talents, opportunities and resources of entrepreneurs) are known to bring about employment creation, provide jobs for women and youth, spread the returns of economic development, help develop rural areas, mobilise domestic savings for investment, inculcate new skills and infuse new technology, and contribute to social and political stability.

MSMEs have been responsible for the rapid growth of economies around the world, historically beginning with the UK and America, gradually to Europe, Latin America and most recently in vast parts of

South and East Asia. Currently, more than 90% of all enterprises in the world are estimated to be MSMEs, accounting for up to 80% of total employment prospects. In OECD countries, the MSME component is as high as 97% of total business activity, contributing between 40% and 60% of GDP in member countries. These statistics hide a plethora of ideas for Africa's economic development targets. First among them is the fact that wholesome MSME growth is fundamental to the expansion of rural economies as part of sustained macroeconomic development.

MSMEs comprise a diverse mix of agriculture-based production, services and trade enterprises; they are classified on the basis of asset value and employee base on a given scale of maximum and minimum scores for both counts. They often represent an extreme variety in terms of size and structure, right from rural artisan guilds, through to small machine shops, emerging software and IT firms. They are by definition dynamic and comprise a wide range of growth-oriented skill sets, with special needs in terms of innovative solutions, technology and equipment and knowledgeable skilled manpower. The central requirement in promoting them is the development of a viable micro-finance industry with built-in ease of access for small and medium enterprises.

Entrepreneurship and Africa's Economic Future

The importance of entrepreneurship to Africa is well recognised. World Bank analysts' argue: "The encouragement of small and medium enterprises in both rural and urban areas should be a high priority in Africa, not only for the development impact of a growing indigenous private sector, but also as a recruiting and training process for future entrepreneurs." (Marsden and Belot) This supportive relationship between the government and entrepreneurs, between the public sector and the non-corporate private sector is what we have in mind when we speak of entrepreneurialism.

In Nigeria, as across the African continent, the majority of the MSMEs established by the country's entrepreneurs are located in the "informal" sector of the economy. This sector provides a wide range of retail products and services for Nigeria's economy. Most MSMEs are small, sole proprietor or family businesses, largely "subsistence" in nature, that market their goods and services to urban and rural consumers. This is necessary entrepreneurship. The small-scale industries, launched by individual entrepreneurs, are the force keeping the local economies within much of Africa going. Arts, crafts, and indigenous textiles, remain important industries in villages and small towns. Tourism is also a significant service industry within many countries in Africa.

There are also the "vibrant" larger scale entrepreneurial enterprises, employing non-family workers and constantly seeking opportunities to expand their operations. MSMEs provide the basis of economic survival for a major part of Nigeria's population. It has been estimated that taken all together the informal sector accounts for more than 70% of the country's economic output (Obadina). It should also be noted that next to agriculture the informal sector is the largest employer of women in most African countries (Soetan). Yet this non-corporate, un-incorporated business sector remains largely unrecorded by state structures responsible for regulating, taxing and providing services to private business. Observers of Nigeria's economy argue that:

> African countries have stocks of raw entrepreneurial talent in small and medium scale enterprises which with training, technology and a supportive political environment, can evolve into capable managers and successful industrialists able to compete globally. ... With respect to a country like Nigeria ... we ... find examples of industries and services that are doing quite well but exist outside the radar of government statisticians (Obadina).

Others argue that the informal sector has the potential to "Generate a large volume of employment at low capital cost. Develop rural Nigeria, and Contribute to gross domestic product." (Obara and Ukpai).

As Nigeria pursues various economic development plans including the National Economic Empowerment and Development Strategy (NEEDS), the Millennium Development Goals (MDGs), and Vision2020, a core part of the national strategy must be to grow and strengthen the vibrant elements of the MSME, largely informal, business sector. As a nation Nigeria, and Africa as a whole, must – cannot afford not to – invest in MSMEs. Their economic future depends on it. The comments and policy commitments of President Paul Kagame of Rwanda should be noted. He has declared "entrepreneurship is the surest way" for Rwanda and Africa to develop. Kagame tells us:

> In the old Rwanda, everyone looked for a job in government because of the benefits and the security. But nowadays they are thinking that the private sector holds the promise of a better life for their families and themselves. More meaningfully, I think that it is better if they join the private sector because there are more opportunities, opportunities that have a higher pay-back than simply working for the public sector. I believe that this is a huge step forward for Rwandans, given our history, given the whole history of Africa. (Kagame)

The genuineness of these words is manifested in the fact that in September 2009 Rwanda was named the world's top business reformer by the International Finance Corporation of the World Bank. The annual report *Doing Business 2010* states "for the first time a Sub-Saharan African economy, Rwanda, is the world's top reformer of business regulation, making it easier to start businesses, register property, protect investors, trade across borders, and access credit." (IFC/World Bank)

In order to go about the business of enterprise start-up and growth, entrepreneurs need a supportive, conducive social and political environment. They need governments that encourage and facilitate entrepreneurship; they need an economic system that rewards the risk-taker and innovator, they will also benefit from a culture that respects and champions the entrepreneur.

Poverty in Africa
Poverty is pervasive throughout the African continent. Outside of the relatively prosperous North Africa countries, 50% of Africa's sub-Saharan population survives on the local equivalents of U.S. $1.25 a day; 70% survive on less than $2 per day.

Poverty head-count ratio at $1.25 a day (PPP) (% of population)

East Asia & Pacific	16.8%	2005
Europe & Central Asia	3.7%	2005
Latin America & Caribbean	8.2%	2005
Middle East & North Africa	3.6%	2005
South Asia	40.3%	2005
Sub-Saharan Africa	50.9%	2005

Poverty head-count ratio at $2 a day (PPP) (% of population)

East Asia & Pacific	38.7%	2005
Europe & Central Asia	8.9%	2005
Latin America & Caribbean	17.1%	2005
Middle East & North Africa	16.9%	2005
South Asia	73.9%	2005
Sub-Saharan Africa	72.9%	2005

Source: World Bank, Data: Poverty Headcount Ratios
http://data.worldbank.org/topic/poverty
Poverty is more than just a lack of income. As detailed by the African Development Bank, poverty is a combination of:

- Persistent hunger and malnutrition and lack of adequate shelter.

- Not being able to obtain medical care when sick.

- Losing children and family members to illness brought by preventable diseases.

- The inability to go to school, read, write or speak properly.

- The need to travel long distances, on foot, to purchase inputs, sell outputs, seek employment or fetch water and fire wood.

- High income and gender-based inequality and the fear of the future due to the feeling of powerlessness, lack of representation as well as lack of freedom and hope. (African Development Bank)

Poverty has a multiplying effect which includes social divisiveness, crime, violence, and political instability. These all impede the ability of the continent's economies to grow, diversify and realise their potential. It is now broadly recognised that one of the keys to poverty alleviation in Africa is private sector development, focusing on support for Africa's informal sector of the numerous MSMEs that sustain the vast majority of the continent's population.

This book presents a comprehensive view of entrepreneurialism in Africa. It provides information on how to become an entrepreneur, the possibilities, advantages and challenges of entrepreneurship, and appropriate entrepreneur-friendly, entrepreneurship-facilitating government policies. The book promotes the entrepreneurial revolution as an economic necessity for Nigeria and the whole of the African continent. It encourages and exhorts you to pursue your entrepreneurial aspirations. In doing this you will be part of the entrepreneurial revolution, and, thereby, the drive to alleviate poverty in Africa. In the next chapter, the discussion presents a concise historical overview of Africa's economy, highlighting the role of entrepreneurship.

Sources

African Development Bank, "Bank Group Policy on Poverty Reduction" February, 2004
http://www.afdb.org/fileadmin/uploads/afdb/Documents/Policy-Documents/10000028-EN-BANK-GROUP-POLICY-ON-POVERTY-REDUCTION.PDF

Baumol, William J.; Litan, Robert E.; and Schramm, Carl J. (2007) "Sustaining Entrepreneurial Capitalism," *Capitalism and Society*: Vol.2: Iss. 2, Article 1. http://www.bepress.com/cas/vol2/iss2/art1 accessed June 18, 2010

Branson, Richard. *Business Stripped Bare: Adventures of a Global Entrepreneur.* London: Virgin Books, 2009.

Di-Masi, Paul. "Defining Entrepreneurship." (www.gdrc.org/icm/micro/define-micro.html accessed June 12, 2010

Entrepreneur.com."Entrepreneur." http://www.entrepreneur.com/encyclopedia/term/159078.html accessed June 12, 2010

Food and Agriculture Organization. "Rural Development through Entrepreneurship." http://www.fao.org/docrep/w6882e/w6882e02.htm#P62_10289, accessed June 13, 2010

Hupalo, Peter I. "Entrepreneur: What's In a Definition?" (www.thinkinglike.com/Essays/entrepreneur-definition.html accessed June 12, 2010

Kaufmann, Friedrich, Philip Madelung, Julius Spatz, Mattia Wegmann. "Business Climate Surveys: Experiences from Ghana, Mozambique, and South Africa." Transparency International, U4Brief February 2008 - No. 4.
Kotelnikov, Vadim. "Entrepreneur." www.1000ventures.com/business.../entrepreneur_main.html accessed June 12, 2010

Marsden, Keith and Therese Belot. *Private Enterprise in Africa: Creating a Better Environment.* World Bank Discussion Papers, 17, 1987

Nawaz, Farzana. "Corruption in fast-growing markets: lessons from Russia and Vietnam." Transparency International, U4 Expert Answer, 29 April, 2008,

http://www.u4.no/helpdesk/helpdesk/query.cfm?id=166, accessed
June 17, 2010

Obama, Barack. *State of the Union Address*. 27 January, 2010

Obara, Lawyer and Ukpai, Ndukwe "Cost Accounting Practice in the
Informal Sector of Nigeria,"
African Training and Research Centre in Administration for
Development,
http://unpan1.un.org/intradoc/groups/public/documents/cafrad/unpan
017691.pdf, accessed July 26, 2010

Organisation for Economic Co-operation and Development, *OECD
Territorial Reviews : Competitive Cities : a New Entrepreneurial
Paradigm in Spatial Development.* Paris: OECD, 2007

Schumpeter J.A. (1975). Theory of Economic Development.
Cambridge, Mass.: Havard
University. orig. pub. 1936.

Small Business Administration. *About the SBA*
http://www.sba.gov/aboutsba/index.html, accessed June 13, 2010.

Tan, Wee-Liang. "Entrepreneurialism: It's Time for a Clearer
Definition." *Journal of Small Business and Entrepreneurship*. 13, 1,
Spring 1996.

Transparency International. *Regional Pages: Africa and the Middle
East*
http://www.transparency.org/regional_pages/africa_middle_east/sub_
saharan_africa, accessed June 17, 2010

Wadhwa, Vivek, et al. *The Anatomy of an Entrepreneur: Making of a
Successful Entrepreneur.*
Kansas City, Missouri: Ewing Marion Kauffman Foundation, 2009.

CHAPTER TWO

AFRICA'S ECONOMIC HISTORY AND ASPIRATIONS

"A lot of people have ideas, but there are few who decide to do something about them now. Not tomorrow. Not next week. But today. The true entrepreneur is a doer, not a dreamer."

Nolan Bushnell, founder of Atari and Chuck E. Cheese's

Africa's Economic History

Although Africa's history is richly interlaced with the entrepreneurial spirit, the continent has been unable to, as a whole, emerge prosperous. Comprised of 54 independent nations, Africa is the second-largest continent in the world, after Asia. The population of Africa circa 2010 is estimated at just over 1 billion, approximately 13 percent of the world's population.

Early Africans were primarily hunters and gatherers; however, by 3000 B.C. the merged empire of Egypt was already bustling with industry and distribution, on a path to distinguish itself as one of the greatest civilisations in history. Early production in Egypt included goods such as papyrus, or paper, and herbal medicines. These developed to include the sale of intellectual services such as writing, astronomical reading, architecture, and other fields during the height of Ancient Egypt.

Around 400 AD, several powerful empires rose up in Western Africa. Historically, the empire of Ghana (Wagadugu) was located in present-day Chad, Sudan, Mali and Senegal before eventually moving south to the coastal areas of West Africa. Ghana built its wealth around gold, establishing mines to unearth the natural resource abundant in the West Africa region. Artisans within this region produced beautiful jewellery from this gold, creating an industry that helped to contribute to its status as a wealthy and powerful kingdom. On a smaller scale, items such as leather and other metal ornaments were also traded. The empire of Ghana developed an elaborate trading system with peoples in North Africa, and beginning around 800 AD, with Arabs to the east and the north.

Around 1200 AD, a new West African power, the empire of Mali, rose to prominence and outperformed Ghana in both riches and power. At the height of its power in the mid-14th century, Mali controlled the Gold-Salt trade throughout much of North and West

Africa. While much of the gold came from sub-Saharan Africa, salt came from northern states such as Morocco and Algeria. Two Malian cities became the centres of trade, Djenne and Timbuktu.

Beyond goods, trading in the early empires in Africa facilitated the spread of ideas, new technologies, inventions, and religion (Islam) from one part of Africa to another. During the height of the Malian empire, Islamic teachings spread rapidly, creating the dominant Muslim populations evident in many North and West African countries today. During the decline of the empire of Mali, the Hausa states and the Ashanti Kingdom, along with the Songhai empire, became powerful. The Ashanti tribe of Ghana became famous for craftsmanship in gold, ivory, textiles, and iron.

The most powerful kingdom that rose to power in Central Africa was the Kongo which emerged about 200 years after the height of the Mali empire. The Kongo's rise to empire status was fuelled by its production and trade of metals, namely copper and iron.

Trans-Saharan Trade Routes

For hundreds of years, the coastal city of Carthage (Tunisia) was the main trading centre of the Mediterranean world, until it engaged in the Punic Wars against Rome and was destroyed in 146 BC. Approximately two centuries later, the Roman Empire had secured control of the entire African coast from Morocco to Egypt. Much later, around 646 AD, Arab armies, spreading the new Islamic religion invaded North Africa and quickly gained control over trade, and used it to spread religion across the Sahara and deep into West and East Africa. Hence trade in Africa consisted largely of interactions with Mediterranean and Arabs nations.

Europe got back in the game when in the late 15th century Vasco da Gama's voyage around Africa opened trade routes for Portugal. Special trading routes were created by the Portuguese to carry goods including iron and captives (slaves) from the interior of the Kongo and the Atlantic coastline. Soon, other European states joined and iron and captives were exported to obtain foreign luxuries and tools such as wool and even guns (History, 200).

With the discovery of the American territories by Europeans, continental trading between Africa and the rest of the world began to shift – leading to Africa's import-heavy economic condition today. Drought-resistant and high-yield crops, like cassava and maize from America, were introduced to kingdoms like Kongo, and quickly became major crops, to the point of replacing the indigenous African millet. Also enslaved Africans became the dominant trade as they were used to work the farmlands of the Americas.

Illegitimate Trade in Captive Africans

Beginning in the late 1400s, the trading of slaves began to transform the face of African trade. Known as Maafa, the Swahili word for holocaust, nearly four hundred years of slave trading led to the displacement of over twelve million Africans. While some of the slaves were captured directly by Europeans who raided cities and kidnapped Africans, another element of the slave trade was the selling of Africans by other Africans.

The Trans-Atlantic Slave Trade is said to have been initiated by the Portuguese, whose interests in Africa's resources shifted from gold to an even more profitable commodity: a cheap labour force. With many of the Native American populations severely sickened with diseases brought by Europeans, and Europeans fatigued by the New World's climate, the Africans were viewed as the ideal, experienced workers. By the 1600s, Europeans had found ways to make every stage of the journey profitable for merchants, a system that became known as the Triangular Trade. In addition to the majority of profits reaching European and American pockets, slave traders also provided opportunity for Africans to profit from the slave trade, by selling their captives.

Most of the slaves sold by the kingdom of Congo were bought by Portuguese slave traders, who then shipped the imprisoned Africans to colonies in Brazil. The Ashanti Kingdom of West Africa (present-day Ghana, Cote d'Ivoire, and Togo) gained significant parts of its empire's wealth by participation in the slave trade by selling men captured in local battles to European slave traders. However, the money earned by African empires from the slave trade pales in comparison to the enormous wealth and infrastructure gained by Americans and Europeans who utilised the free labour of slaves.

Imperialism and Colonialism

Because of its proximity to Europe, North Africa was subject to invasion from the time of the earliest civilisations. Phoenicians, Greeks, Romans, and others discovered, explored, defeated, and even settled in parts of North Africa as early as 800 BC.

Following this pattern, Europeans began to explore more deeply the interior of the African continent in the 1800s. Scottish explorer, David Livingstone became the first European to cross the continent from East to West. Later that century, rivalries between white settlers extended into competition and led to seizing of the land by European nations. Many Africans, though they resisted, were not able to combat the modern weapons of the Europeans. The French focused on North and West Africa, the British on West, South and East Africa, Egypt, and Sudan, the Portuguese on the Western, South-western and South-eastern coasts. In addition, the Belgians established a foothold in today's Democratic Republic of the Congo. Dutch settlers moved into South Africa and the Germans claimed some territories in West, East and South Africa.

Much of Nigeria was owned and ruled by George Goldie's National Africa Company, chartered by the British government; it ruthlessly exploited thousands of square miles and dominated hundreds of thousands of Africans. Like other colonial controllers, Goldie did not care much for ethical business codes, fair trade, or transparency and so like the others, laid the foundation for state corruption in the African region today. The colonial states were created with the sole or primary purpose of extracting commodities for Europe. They did so as cheaply as possible and, as a result, they made their ruler-owners wealthy.

For example, Britain from its colonies in Africa, extracted raw materials, processed them, and exported them back to the continent in the cheapest manner to maximise its profits. The discovery of diamonds and gold in South Africa, as well as the belief that Africa had unlimited quantities of raw materials effectively led to a "scramble for Africa" by European powers, which propagated conflict and wars – the remnants of which still plague the continent today. To reduce their competition, European powers, along with the United States of America, met in Berlin from 1884-1885 to divide Africa among themselves. Carving out their spheres of rule and dominance, they created artificial boundaries with no consideration to the needs or desires of the African people.

Financial Turmoil Caused by Colonisation

European colonisation of Africa created ill-structured economic systems, mono-crop export-oriented trade, and widespread poverty. Because European colonialists were interested only in commodities and raw materials, the colonies did not develop diversified economic systems. Dependence on agricultural products and minerals meant that African countries were subject to external pricing and demand. Additionally, the extreme climates within Africa, such as drought, could lead quickly to famine and loss of production. Lack of health and education systems also hindered Africa's potential for economic growth.

During the colonial era, entrepreneurship in Africa was dominated by the colonial rulers while local entrepreneurs could participate only as suppliers to the colonial machine. Manufacturing was generally at small scale levels supplemented in some colonies by relatively complex industries producing mainly for export, and food, fibre and wood processing, and metal works in order to meet the needs of fast growing urban populations (William T., 2004).

Natural resources were selected and exploited with a view to meeting the needs of the industries in Western Europe. To this end, infrastructure, particularly all-weather roads and railroads were designed and built with the aim of facilitating the shipment of minerals and agricultural commodities from the hinterland to the seaports for purposes of further shipment overseas. Other components of the colonial economy such as banking and communication were mainly established to facilitate this end.

Resistance to Colonialism and Post-Colonisation

Through the periods of imperialism and colonialism by Europeans, only one nation remained fully independent: Ethiopia. When invaded by Italy in 1935, Ethiopia drove the soldiers out, setting an example for other Africans. Liberia, which was founded in 1847 by returning emancipated slaves, also remained independent. Post 1945 brought an awakening to colonised African states who began to demand an end to colonialism. Many of the would-be freedom-fighters and statesmen had been forced to fight for their colonial masters in the World Wars and tens of thousands were killed.

The struggles of these visionaries came to fruition in the 1960s when the majority of African countries gained independence. From the onset, these newly independent countries launched ambitious plans both independently and regionally, to promote economic growth. For example, Kwame Nkrumah, first prime minister (1957-1960) and then president (1960-1966) of Ghana favoured a socialist development model rather than a capitalist model. Nkrumah tried to speedily develop the Ghanaian economy by embarking on capital intensive projects and social development schemes. Between 1961 and 1966, he built Akosombo Dam, Cocoa Manufacturing Plant, Tema Industrial Township, University of Cape Coast, a sugar factory, a nuclear plant, and other projects. On the continental front, Nkrumah is best known for his unwavering commitment to and advancement of Pan-Africanism. He was instrumental in the founding of the Organisation of African Unity (now African Union) in 1963.

Alongside the OAU, several economic regional blocs where formed to induce co-operation amongst African states and development within bloc members. The blocs include: East African Community (1967; 2000), Economic Community of West African States (1975), and Southern Africa Development Community (formerly Southern African Development Co-ordinating Conference; 1980). These regional blocs epitomised the dreams of Africa's founding fathers to create a prosperous and thriving continent.

Indeed, the post-colonial destinies of individual countries as well as the continent were shaped by the political ideology of notable leaders including Kwame Nkrumah (Ghana), Sekou Toure (Guinea), Houphouët-Boigny (Cote d'Ivoire), Jomo Kenyatta (Kenya), Patrice Lumumba (Congo), Nnamdi Azikiwe (Nigeria), and Julius Nyerere (Tanzania).

Throughout Africa, the first decades of independence were characterised by centralised leadership and state-driven economic progress. Buildings of roads, schools, corporations, and social facilities were typical as was a rigid separation between public and private enterprise.   Thus, while one may characterise this early period of African independence as an enjoyment of economic growth, one must also acknowledge the dichotomy between public and private enterprise whereby public enterprise was promoted and private enterprise neglected. Further, African economies continued to be dominated by former colonists and developed economies of Britain, France, Portugal, and United States.

Facing extreme poverty following the first decade of independence, African countries borrowed billions of dollars from banks in Europe and the United States in order to pay for development, but many of these products fell short of their goals or were managed by corrupt leaders, and countries were left even poorer and in greater debt. Today, Africa remains the world's poorest continent, producing only two percent of the world's gross domestic product, even though it houses approximately 13 percent of the world's population.

Since independence, the majority of African nations have been crippled by civil war or conflict at one time or another. Forty military coups have rocked the continent in the last three decades. Some of Africa's countries are still suffering under long-standing wars today. Needless to say, wars prevent much of the entrepreneurial growth potential of African countries.

Today's Principal Commercial Products

Despite Africa being the poorest continent, it possesses rich and fertile soils, and perhaps most importantly, a young and entrepreneurial work force. During the 1980s and 1990s, African nations found themselves under intense pressure to reform their economies and establish free markets. While some argue that this system only enriches the lives of a few, others debate that not enough time has passed to fully understand how free markets are transforming the lives of Africans and their communities.

The resource endowments of African countries include:

Agricultural and Mineral Resources - African Countries

Source: African Studies Center, Michigan State University,
"Exploring Africa: Africa's Natural Resources"
http://exploringafrica.matrix.msu.edu/teachers/curriculum/m6/natural
_resources.html

Country	Agriculture	Mineral
ALGERIA	wheat, oats, olives	Petroleum
ANGOLA	coffee, bananas, maize	petroleum, diamonds
BENIN	coffee, cocoa, yams	Petroleum
BOTSWANA	maize, sorghum, livestock	diamonds
BURKINA FASO	ground nuts, cotton, sorghum	manganese, limestone
BURUNDI	coffee, cotton, maize	Gold
CAMEROON	coffee, cocoa, cassava	petroleum, aluminum
CAPE VERDE	bananas, maize, fish	Salt
CENTRAL AFRICAN REBULIC	cassava, millet, cotton	Diamonds
CHAD	cotton, millet, sorghum	Uranium
COMOROS	vanilla, copra, bananas, fish	
CONGO (Brazzaville)	rice, groundnuts, maize	petroleum, diamonds
CONGO (Kinshasa)	cassava, maize, coffee, rubber	copper, diamonds, cobalt, gold, zinc
COTE D'IVOIRE	coffee, cocoa, timber, maize, rice	petroleum, diamonds, manganese
DJIBOUTI	sheep, goats, fruit	
EGYPT	cotton, rice, maize, fruit	petroleum, iron ore, phosphates
EQUATORIAL GUINEA	timber, coffee, rice, yams	petroleum
ERITREA	sorghum, lentils, fish, livestock	gold, potash, zinc
ETHIOPIA	coffee, tiv, pulses, livestock	gold, , copper
GABON	cocoa, coffee, oil palm, cassava	petroleum, manganese
GAMBIA	groundnuts, millet, sorghum, rice	
GHANA	cocoa, cassava, groundnuts, maize	gold, bauxite, manganese
GUINEA	rice, coffee, pineapples, cassava	bauxite, iron ore, uranium
GUINEA-BISSAU	rice, maize, cassava, fish	bauxite, phosphates
LESOTHO	livestock, maize, sorghum	water (hydro)

Country	Agriculture	Mineral
LIBERIA	rubber, timber, rice, cassava	iron ore, diamonds
LIBYA	wheat, olives, dates	petroleum, gypsum
MADAGASCAR	coffee, vanilla, sugar, timber	graphite, chromite, coal, bauxite
MALAWI	tobacco, tea, maize, cassava	Limestone
MALI	cotton, livestock, millet, rice	gold, phosphates
MAURITANIA	fish, livestock, millet, rice	iron ore, gypsum, copper
MOROCCO	wheat, barley, citrus, dates	phosphates, iron ore, manganese
MOZAMBIQUE	cotton, cashew nuts, maize, cassava	coal, titanium
NAMIBIA	millet, sorghum, livestock	diamonds, copper, uranium, gold
NIGER	cotton, millet, sorghum, cassava	uranium, coal, iron ore
NIGERI A	cocoa, groundnuts, palm oil, maize, sorghum	petroleum, tin, columbite, iron ore
RWANDA	coffee, tea, sorghum, beans, bananas	gold, tin ore
SAO TOME & PRINCIPE	fish, palm kernels, bananas	
SENEGAL	cotton, groundnuts, sorghum, rice	phosphates, iron ore
SEYCHELLES	coconuts, cinnamon, vanilla, cassava	
SIERRA LEONE	rice, coffee, palm kernels	diamonds, bauxite, iron ore
SOMALIA	bananas, sorghum, fruits, livestock	Uranium
SOUTH AFRICA	maize, wheat, sugar, fruits, livestock, poultry	gold, diamonds, uranium, chromium
SUDAN	cotton, sorghum, millet	petroleum, iron ore, copper
SWAZILAND	sugar, maize, fruits, timber	asbestos, coal, clay
TANZANIA	coffee, tea, cotton, maize, cassava	tin, phosphates, iron ore, diamonds
TOGO	coffee, cocoa, yams, cassava, maize	phosphates, limestone
TUNISIA	olives, dates, citrus, wheat	petroleum, phosphates, iron ore
UGANDA	coffee, tea, cassava, maize, bananas	copper, cobalt
WESTERN SAHARA	fish, livestock	phosphates, iron ore
ZAMBIA	maize, sorghum, groundnuts	copper, cobalt, zinc, lead
ZIMBABWE	cotton, tobacco, maize, livestock	coal, chromium ore, asbestos

Despite its impressive natural resources, Africa's economy lacks diversity. Oil, minerals and agricultural products account for 80% of exports. (African Economic Outlook) Africa's principal exports today are agricultural products. Coffee, cocoa, pineapples, coconuts and palm oil remain the most significant exports. Cotton is also a significant source of income for a number of North and West African countries, while cashews, vanilla beans and cloves are produced for export in East Africa. In countries such as Kenya and Cote d'Ivoire, fresh flowers are grown, then cut and shipped on planes to Europe. While fishing remains an important source of income for people along the coastal areas, much of the catch is for local consumption.

Irrespective of being rich in petroleum and minerals, many of the West and Central African wars have been fuelled in part by competition over diamonds, gold or oil. Moreover, because the prices of many exports are controlled by international markets with fluctuating daily prices, revenues for Africans are constantly subjected to unpredictable up and down swings. In addition to these industries, which are often controlled by huge corporations, Africa is abundant in platinum, copper, cobalt, zinc, bauxite, uranium, iron ore, and phosphates. Reflecting the limited level of industrial production and the growing demand for food, Africa's main imports are machinery and equipment, chemicals, petroleum products, scientific instruments, and foodstuffs.

In more recent history, industry has begun to play a more significant role in some of Africa's larger countries. Northern African countries are manufacturers of petrochemical and pharmaceutical products. Some African countries house large aluminium and steel mills, although most of these production facilities in smaller nations only output enough steel for national use. Contemporary textiles are produced in factories throughout Africa as well. Food and beverage production is a growing industry, with many countries producing local beer or soft drinks that are under license to international companies.

Wines are made in a few African countries as well, namely South Africa and Morocco.

Growing in extent since the independence era, Asian countries such as China have increasingly saturated African marketplaces with cheaply imported goods, providing a host of modern conveniences ranging from plastic buckets to digital music players. In some West African countries, even the staple meal, rice, is primarily imported from Southeast Asian countries such as Vietnam. Although the development of several regional Fair Trade Organisations have encouraged the sustainable, local production and export of foods and goods, the agricultural and manufacturing entrepreneurial movement concerned with justice and sustainability is still in its infancy. According to the Fair Trade Federation, fairly traded products worldwide still account for less than one percent of all goods traded between underdeveloped and developed nations.

It may be observed that since independence, the African continent is, in general, a latecomer and marginal actor in the current international economy. One area of weakness is the continent's inability to pursue entrepreneurial development in a concerted manner. Throughout the 1960s through to the 1990s, the international economic system was under the control of the developed countries of the North under the General Agreement on tariffs and Trade (GATT) arrangement. This system generally failed to treat African countries as equal players in the international economic system. By the same token, the World Trade Organisation (WTO), which was formed in 1994 to replace the GATT, has also failed to create an equitable environment for Africa's farmers and manufacturers.

Africa's industrialisation woes cannot entirely be blamed on the North. African regional integration seemed compromised right from the start. The OAU Charter of May 1963 was itself a compromise arrangement. A group of African leaders led by Kwame Nkrumah, Julius Nyerere and Sekou Toure of Guinea wished that Africa would be united as one country – the United States of Africa. However, the majority of leaders preferred the formation of sub-regional groupings which would, over time, pursue the dream of a united Africa. On a critical note, most of these sub-regional groupings – the East African Community (EAC), the Economic Community of West African States (ECOWAS), the Southern African Development Co-ordination Conference (SADCC), the Maghreb Union among others – did not manage to deliver the Pan-African dream, let alone secure any formidable economic development among the member states. In recent years, some of these organisations have evolved economic integration policies which sought to boost industrialisation among member states through common policies in customs and excise, fiscal planning, regional development, trade and industry, central banking and immigration. Despite such moves, these organisations have been unable to engender any significant industrial growth among African countries.

Summary

Entrepreneurship activities bring about business and production innovation with resultant growth in enterprises and industrial organisations. From history, entrepreneurship development in Africa is a late starter as the indigenous entrepreneurs were never allowed to develop by the colonial entrepreneurs. For the time being, African entrepreneurs have ventured into the less-explored areas of telecom, transport, hospitality, music, film and food processing. Governments of African countries (e.g. Nigeria) have supported entrepreneurial ingenuity through various programs to encourage self employment, income empowerment, social cohesion, technical progress and economic development. Much more needs to be done, however, to bring about the necessary entrepreneurial revolution. Entrepreneurship development still remains the strong policy option for developing Africa's manufacturing and industrial sectors. With increase in support from governments of African countries, the

African Union and its Regional Economic Communities, exploration of new areas of competitive and natural advantage by entrepreneurs, among others, Africa will stand a better chance of increasing her pace of economic development and becoming a force to reckon with economically.

The next chapter takes a closer look at Nigeria as a case study of the challenges and opportunities for entrepreneurialism, economic growth and poverty alleviation.

Sources

Africa. Http://en.wikipedia.org/wiki/africa accessed on July 7, 2010.

African Economic Outlook, "The 60-second Guide," http://www.africaneconomicoutlook.org/fileadmin/uploads/aeo/Reso urces/...pdf

Dickovick, J. Tyler, Ph.D. *Africa.* 43rd Edition. Harper's Ferry, WV: Stryker-Post Publications, 2008.

Dowden, Richard. *Africa: Altered States, Ordinary Miracles*. New York: Perseus Books, Public Affairs, 2009.

Habeeb, William Mark. *Africa: Facts and Figures*. Philadelphia: Mason Crest Publishers, 2005.

Heinrichs, Ann. *Nigeria.* New York: Scholastic, Children's Press, 2010.
Ketena, Makonnen, The Creation of the OAU, at http://www.oau-creation.com/creation_of_the_oau_1.htm, accessed July 10, 2010.
Kwame Nkrumah (1909-1972),
http://www.lsu.edu/student_organizations/aso/nkrumah.htm, accessed on July 7, 2010.

Legum, C. *Africa since Independence* Indianapolis, Indiana University Press, 1999.

Mboya T. *The Challenge of Development in Contemporary African Monographs, The Challenge Development* East Africa Foundation Publishers, 1968.

Nzau, Mamu, "Africa's Industrialization Debate: A Critical Analysis, *The Journal of Language, Technology & Entrepreneurship in Africa,* Vol. 2. No.1. 2010, ISSN 1998-1279. http://ajol.info/index.php/jolte/article/viewFile/51996/40631, accessed July 2010.

Pakenham, Thomas. *The Scramble for Africa*. New York: Random House, 1991.

Rodney, W. *How Europe Underdeveloped Africa*. Heinemann, Nairobi, 1989.

Shillington, Kevin. *History of Africa*. New York: McMillan, rev. 2005.

UNFPA. *State of World Population 2009*. United Nations Population Fund. New York, NY 10017, 2009.

William T. *Government and politics in Africa* Macmillan Houndmills, Basingtoke, London, 2004.

CHAPTER THREE

NIGERIA'S ECONOMY AND ENTREPRENEURIAL DEVELOPMENT

"The time is always right to do the right thing."

Martin Luthur King Jr

"The future belongs to those who believe in the beauty of their dreams."

Eleanor Roosevelt

Despite the hundreds of billion of dollars earned by Nigeria's exports of oil and gas over the past four decades, many of the basic measures of social and economic development have shown little, if any, improvement. The link between Nigeria's history and the current economic reality is that the country continues to be overwhelmingly a supplier of raw materials with a large traditional non-commercial agricultural base. The manufacturing sector is underdeveloped and marginal. Nigeria's population is largely sustained by the informal sector, petty trading, economic activity. The economy is increasingly dependent upon imports of food, consumer and capital goods. Human development indicators place Nigeria squarely in the bottom 20% of surveyed countries. How do we explain these realities? Why has there been no profound break with the economic past? What does the country need to do to transform itself and realise its potential? If Nigeria is to seize its opportunities, if it is to provide sustainable livelihoods for its burgeoning population, if it is to quell social unrest and provide a stake in the economy for marginalised women and youth, if it is to reach its vaunted Vision 2020 goal of becoming the world's 20th largest economy by the year 2020, then the country must encourage the entrepreneurial energies of its people. It must undergo an entrepreneurial revolution.

An Overview of Nigeria's Economy

Based on 2009 World Bank gross domestic product nominal data, Nigeria's economy is currently the third largest in Africa (after South Africa and Egypt) and the 44th largest in the world. Previously Nigeria ranked second to South Africa. Using IMF gross domestic product purchasing power parity data, Nigeria ranks as Africa's 3rd the world's 37th largest economy. Over the past decade Nigeria's economy has grown on average 8% per annum. Even in the current global economic downturn and hesitant recovery, Nigeria's economy grew by 7% in the first quarter of 2010.

Gross Domestic Product, 2009 – World Rankings - Africa's Top 5

of / *192* (*World Bank*)	of/180 (IMF)	Economy	GDP - Nominal / GDP - PPP (Millions of US dollars)	
31	25	South Africa	285,983	492,684
42	26	Egypt, Arab Rep.	188,334	442,640
44	**37**	**Nigeria**	**168,994**	**315,401**
50	47	Algeria	140,577	233,098
57	57	Morocco	90,859	136,728

Sources: World Development Indicators database, World Bank, 1 July 2010
http://siteresources.worldbank.org/DATASTATISTICS/Resources/GDP.pdf
IMF statistics reported in Wikipedia, "List of Countries by GDP (PPP),"
http://en.wikipedia.org/wiki/List_of_countries_by_GDP_(PPP) 29 July, 2010

Key comparative population, landmass and GDP purchasing power parity indices for Nigeria include:

Basic Indicators, 2009 – Selected African and Referent Countries
(Refer to diagram on next page)

	Population (thousands)	Land area (thousands of km^2)	GDP/PPP valuation (US $ millions)	GDP per capita (PPP valuation, $)	Annual real GDP growth (average % 2001-2009)
Africa	1,000,345	30,323	2,825,691	2,802	5.3
Nigeria	*154,729*	*924*	*327,822*	*2,119*	*8.2*
Algeria	34,895	2,382	256,542	7,352	3.7
Botswana	1,950	582	25,764	13,214	3.9
Cote d'Ivoire	21,075	322	33,766	1,602	0.9
Egypt	82,999	1,001	471,509	5,681	4.9
Ethiopia	82,825	1,104	72,196	872	8.0
Ghana	23,837	239	36,558	1,534	5.5
Kenya	39,802	593	62,423	1,568	4.1
Senegal	12,534	197	20,841	1,663	3.8
South Africa	50,110	1,221	487,107	9,721	3.6
Tanzania	43,739	945	53,167	1,216	6.9
Zimbabwe	12,523	391	2,193	175	-5.4
					(average % 2000-2008)
Brazil	193,262	8,515	2,013,186	10,200	5.0
Russia	141,927	17,098	2,109,551	15,100	5.0
India	1,183,770	3,287	3,526,124	3,100	7.0
China	1,338,890	9,597	8,765,240	6,600	11.0

Oil was first discovered in 1956 at Oloibiri in the Niger Delta; commercial production began in 1958. (NNPC) Coming into a huge fortune of oil and natural gas reserves soon after gaining independence from British colonial rule in 1960, Nigeria's new leadership tipped the economy towards an overwhelming dependence on non-renewable mineral resources. The country profited immensely from the oil boom of the 1970s, but this was accompanied by a simultaneous official, public policy neglect of agriculture and small scale manufacturing. From the early 1980s through the 1990s the Nigerian economy stagnated. Various economic states of economic emergency and macroeconomic adjustment policies were enacted, especially by the administration of President Ibrahim Babangida, intending to restructure the economy. These included currency devaluation, reduction and removal of subsidies on food and energy, retrenchment of government employees, privatisation of parastatals, abandoning of foreign exchange and foreign investment controls, and increased agricultural producer prices.

One of the key effects of the stagnation was the rapid growth of the informal economy. The activities of this sector were largely survivalist, necessity, or subsistence entrepreneurship because of their inherent and almost exclusive dependence on personal initiative, resources and risk-bearing capacity. Currently almost 70% of Nigeria's GDP and 90% of job creation are contributed by informal enterprises. (Kazeem) It is the same informal economy that must be encouraged and supported as the basis of Nigeria's entrepreneurial revolution.

Despite its natural endowments, Nigeria is crippled with rampant poverty and depressing macroeconomic indicators and human development indices. The resulting 'Nigerian Paradox' describes the massive macroeconomic imbalances that have pushed a country brimming with natural and human resources into mass poverty. Successive decades of massive embezzlement have wreaked acute social and economic deprivation on Nigerians, causing the country to lag behind on all socio-economic indices, including infrastructure, health and education. The 2009 UNDP Human Development Index – a composite measure of three dimensions of human development: life expectancy, education and adult literacy, and income – puts Nigeria at the 158th position in a survey of 172 countries. (UNDP) More than 70% of Nigeria's population lives on less than \$1 per day; they live in extreme poverty without access to fundamental necessities. Unemployment and underemployment are endemic. Decades of political turmoil, civilian unrest and large scale government mismanagement and corruption have permitted a continuation of outdated and non-inclusive policies. The term "prebendalism" (Joseph) has been used to denote Nigeria's unique brand of corruption. In a 2000 survey of 90 countries, *Transparency International* ranked Nigeria as the most corrupt in the world. As of 2009, the global Corruption Perception Index (CPI) ranked Nigeria 130 out of 180 reporting counties (Africa Economic Outlook/Transparency International).

Sectors of the Nigerian Economy

A sectoral overview of Nigeria's economy reveals the following data for 2008 and 2009:

Nigeria's Economy - GDP by sector, 2008 (%)

Wholesale and retail trade	15.9
Telecommunication and Post	1.0
Solid Mineral	0.2
Other services	8.2
Manufacturing	2.4
Hotels	0.4
Finance and business services	1.8
Crude petroleum and natural gas	32.3
Construction	1.4
Agriculture	36.5

Source:
http://www.africaneconomicoutlook.org/en/countries/west-africa/nigeria/

Nigeria's Economy - GDP by sector, 2009 (%)

TeleComm/Postal ServicesContributed 3.67% to the GDP in 2009	Solid MineralsContributed 0.38% to the GDP in 2009
ManufacturingContributed 4.19% to the GDP in 2009	Finance & InsuranceContributed 3.71% to the GDP in 2009
Building & ConstructionContributed 1.98% to the GDP in 2009	AgricultureContributed 41.84% to the GDP in 2009
Hotel and RestaurantContributed 0.49% to the GDP in 2009	Wholesale and RetailContributed 18.16% to the GDP in 2009
Crude Petroleum & Natural Gas Contributed 16.05% to the GDP in 2009	OthersContributed 7.04% to the GDP in 2009

Source: National Bureau of Statistics, "News," http://www.nigerianstat.gov.ng/ accessed August 4, 2010

Oil and Gas: A key feature of the Nigerian economy is the high dependence on the capital-intensive oil and gas sector for national revenue generation. The oil sector accounts for over 95 percent of export earnings and 80 percent of government revenues. However, as of 2009, the oil and gas sector accounted for less than 40% of GDP. Nigeria has reaped huge profits from oil exports. Nigeria earns an estimated $100 million every day from oil exports alone; it has proven reserves of over 37 billion barrels in oil and 188 trillion cubic meters of natural gas. Nigeria has the largest known gas reserves in Africa and is also the continent's top crude oil producer at 2.21 million barrels per day. Nigeria exports 40% of its production to the United States, amounting to approximately 10% of US crude petroleum imports; most of the remaining crude is exported to Europe, Brazil and India. (US Energy Information Administration).

A key feature of the oil industry is the militancy of local communities seeking a fairer share of the huge wealth generated by oil and gas, and compensation for the environmental damage, health risks and loss of agricultural and fishing livelihoods caused by the industry. Widespread theft of crude and refined oil from pipelines, and smuggling of petroleum are also notable. Bombings, kidnappings and oil-field raids continue to cause an estimated $1 billion in monthly oil revenue losses. Mounting attacks on the oil infrastructure over the past few years have restricted production to 66% of the installed capacity of 3 million barrels per day. In fact, international observers point out a direct link between these developments and the record high of $150 a barrel that oil prices touched in 2008.

Energy Overview

Proven Oil Reserves (January 1, 2010)	37.2 billion barrels (Oil and Gas Journal)
Oil Production (2009)	2.21 million barrels per day, of which 2.221.8 million bbl was crude oil.
Proven Natural Gas Reserves (January 1, 2010)	188 trillion cubic feet (Oil and Gas Journal)
Natural Gas Production (2008)	1,159 billion cubic feet
Recoverable Coal Reserves (2006)	210 million short tons (World Energy Council)
Coal Production (2008)	0.009 million short tons

Source: http://www.eia.doe.gov/cabs/Nigeria/Profile.html

The dependence on oil revenues has facilitated the endemic problem of the Nigerian economy and the large scale misappropriation of national assets by political and bureaucratic agents. Apart from the petroleum sector, Nigeria's economy is grossly inefficient and human capital is underdeveloped.

Agriculture: Agricultural production is the leading contributor to Nigeria's GDP, and it accounts for over 70% of employment. The sector is labour-intensive and much of the farming is non-commercial. Productivity is low due to generally poor or limited extension services, a lack of modern technology, poor food storage and transportation infrastructure, and the relatively small size of farm holdings. Nigeria is no longer a major exporter of many agricultural products like cocoa, groundnuts, palm oil, corn, millet, rice, rubber, sorghum, etc. Agriculture has failed to keep pace with Nigeria's rapid population growth; hence, Nigeria is a net importer of food, unlike in the 1960s when it was a net exporter. (African economic outlook)

Manufacturing: manufacturing contributes less than 3% to GDP reflecting the low level of industrialisation of the Nigerian economy. This is a sharp decline from the 9.5% contribution to GDP in the early 1980s. Nigeria manufacturing has not been able to take advantage of its large domestic and regional market. Major barriers faced by manufacturers include bad roads, inadequate water supply, erratic power supply, paucity of credit, and poor security for persons and property. Currently, manufacturing activity is concentrated in the major urban centres – Lagos, Kano, Kaduna, Ibadan, and Port Harcourt. Leading products are textiles, beverages, cigarettes, detergents, cement, steel, aluminium, wood pulp, paper, and petrochemicals. (African economic outlook; Wilson)

Finance and Business Services: The financial sector contributes approximately only 2% to GDP. This reflects the fact that this sector is inadequate for the credit and investment needs of the non-corporate private sector. For the most part the banking sector functions to fund government debt and make loans to large scale, well connected enterprises. The insurance and mortgage sectors are very small. MSMEs avoid borrowing from banks as the high level of interest rates is unaffordable. Development financial institutions have made little impact on this lack of credit to the MSME sector. Thus finance for entrepreneurship comes from personal savings and reinvested earnings. This self-financing does not generate significant enterprise growth, rather it locks the vast majority of entrepreneurs into low-investment, essentially subsistence enterprise such as petty trading. This supports the cycle of economic stagnation, wide income inequality, and continued mass poverty. The lack of credit for business start-up and growth also results in constant pressure for government to be the employer of last resort. (King) The need for affordable, adequate financing for the MSME sector is critical if the entrepreneurial revolution is to take hold.

Other Services and Sectors: Wholesale and retail trade, the film industry, and building and construction are also notable contributors to Nigeria's GDP. All these service and production activities are hindered by the business environmental constraints of inadequate infrastructure, policy inconsistencies, insufficient credit, financial irregularities, and security concerns.

A major aspect that is crippling many sectors of Nigeria's economy is endemic corruption, which impedes the development of any economy and hinders prosperity. The Economic Crime and Financial Institution (EFCC) was set up by the Nigerian Government to deal with corruption cases and has made substantial headway in investigations as well as recovery of stolen money. According to the General Manager of the Enterprise Development division of Lagos Business School, Peter Bamkole, corruption is not the main constraint to entrepreneurship; rather, it is a combination of other factors. Bamkole describes the setbacks by denoting them in form of the acronym MISFIT which stands for Market, Infrastructure, Support Services, Information and Technology. Lack of these factors outlined below is said to be the cause of many setbacks in the business.

Market: Not many individuals have sufficient access to large markets and even if they do, they do not understand these markets as well as they should. This issue is even more profound when it comes to international markets which are virtually untapped by many entrepreneurs.

Infrastructure: The absence of stable supply of power, poor roads, congested ports, etc. resulting in high production costs and sub-standard provision of amenities.

Support services: There are very few organisations that offer guidance and mentorship to entrepreneurs who need this service badly.

Finance: Entrepreneurs lack sufficient risk capital sources.

Information: Without sufficient information, business people lack the required motivation and exposure that should be present in any business environment in order to make informed decisions.

Technology: When an entrepreneur does not have the right modern tools to enhance business processes, productivity and efficiency are hindered.

In order to address these issues hindering economic growth and diversification and fostering poverty in Nigeria, there needs to be a concerted effort from all the concerned parties. There must be a shift from the usual inconsistency between pronouncement and the actual implementation of policies. Still, there is much potential in the entrepreneurial sector in Nigeria; it needs to be encouraged by determined, consistent, persistent government policies designed to drive and consolidate an entrepreneurial revolution.

Nigeria's Economy and the Global Economic Meltdown

The global economic meltdown which began in 2008 has had major impacts on the Nigerian economy. This economic crisis severely affected the different facets of the Nigeria economy as well as the performance of the various tiers of government. The crisis is still unfolding and uncertainty exists regarding long-term impacts. It should be stated that Nigeria's economy already faced numerous challenges prior to 2008 related to a fragile financial system, lack of economic diversification, large scale unemployment and underemployment, etc. The global meltdown simply exacerbated the situation. In Nigeria major impacts of crisis can be summarised thus: Declining global economic activity has decreased demand and, therefore, put downward pressure on the prices of traded commodities, including, notably, oil.

Nigerian crude oil, which sold for a record high of $146 per barrel in July 2008 fell to $39 per barrel in January 2009. In July 2010 prices partially recovered to $75 per barrel. (EIA) In the attempt to shore up oil prices, OPEC reduced the daily production allocations of member states. Nigeria's quota dropped from 2.292m bpd to 1.67m bpd. The slow global economic recovery will not, readily, push oil prices back to the record highs of mid-2008. Nigeria's 2010 budget projections are based on an assumed $50 per barrel prices. The fall in both the price of oil and the reduced OPEC quota has had ripple effects throughout the economy. The heavily oil-dependent Nigerian economy has witnessed sharp reductions in government revenues.

This has led to reduced federal and state governments budgetary allocation, resulting in decreased government capital and recurring expenditures, reduced funding of social programmes, decreased government demand for private sector goods and services, public and private sector worker layoffs. Major declines in foreign direct investment (FDI) and withdrawals of equity investments have occurred as investors are focused on financial problems in their home countries. Also waning confidence in the Nigerian economy has spurred investors to switch to more familiar and less volatile equity markets. From March 2008 to February 2009, capitalisation of the Nigerian stock market fell by more than 50%.

The global crisis exacerbated already poor lending practices and risky financial investments of many of Nigeria's banks. In August 2009, five of Nigeria's major banks - Afribank, Intercontinental

Bank, Finbank, Oceanic Bank and Union Bank - had to be bailed out by the Nigerian government to the tune of $2.6 billion. (Global Research) Thousands of bank workers have lost their jobs. This financial sector turmoil has furthered undermined confidence in the economy and made business and investment credit even more scarce. The decrease foreign exchange earnings and stock market volatility have weakened the naira from 117 naira to the dollar in 2008 to 150 naira to the dollar in 2009. This decline in the value of the naira has increased costs of sources consumer and capital goods, and industrial materials.

Increased unemployment in the heavily industrialised economies of Western Europe and North America, have reduced remittances from Nigerians abroad, impacting both disposable income of local recipients and investment funds from the diaspora. The pursuit of Nigeria's Millennium Development Goals (MDG) and the Vision 2020 national development plan are being negatively affected by slower economic growth, reduced foreign exchange earnings, reduced aid funding (ODA), currency depreciation, reduced business credit, and increased unemployment.

In responding to the global economic crisis, Nigeria and similar developing countries will face three main challenges:

1) Economic Stabilisation: The global economic crisis threatens growth, employment and balance of payments stability. Policies must seek to insure the integrity and viability of the financial sector, shore up government revenues, rationalise government expenditures and stabilise exchange rates.

2) Protecting Longer-term Growth and Development: Government should resist the temptation to cutback spending on critical public infrastructure and human resources development.

3) Protecting the Vulnerable: While the broad impacts of the crisis will increase poverty in Nigeria, the reduction in government revenue and budget allocations will undercut poverty alleviation programmes. Government must redouble commitments to help vulnerable sectors of the population, especially women and youth.

Policies for limiting the spread effects of the global crisis, and addressing the already felt impacts on Nigeria must include diversifying the economy from its present overwhelming dependence on the oil and gas sector. There are numerous possibilities for enterprise presented by Nigeria's domestic and regional economies. Many have already been identified. Government policies must centre on encouraging entrepreneurs to pursue these opportunities.

Going Forward: Visions, Resources and Policies

Before leaving office in 2007, outgoing President Olusegun Obasanjo pushed through legislation that made Nigerian university students of all disciplines study entrepreneurship as a mandatory academic subject. The move was part of an ambitious blueprint to take this resource-rich but paradoxically impoverished sub-Saharan nation with a litany of negative indices to the top twenty world economies by 2020. At its core was the ideal of an entrepreneurial revolution that would drive this radical transformation.

The high cost of doing business, infra-structural deficits, lack of credit and relatively unfavourable government policies and practices are among the significant deterrents to entrepreneurial initiatives in Nigeria. In the context of relevant economic strategy, Nigerian policy makers would perhaps do well to borrow from successful Asian models that have displayed rapidly effective results. New Asian "tigers" like Malaysia, Singapore and Thailand have flourished by successfully changing from labour-intensive to capital and technology-intensive businesses to speed up development and attract foreign investments. Significant lessons could also be learnt from Margaret Thatcher's economic policies that propelled Britain to an economic boom in the '80s through extensive promotion of entrepreneurial initiative and share-ownership. Thatcherism's thrust of substituting debt with equity spawned colossal economic development in the UK, which was soon adapted and replicated across Southeast Asia.

Certainly, Africa represents uniquely different realities and challenges, and there is no effective model than can be entirely transplanted here. Policy makers must prioritise institutional efforts to compensate for reigning socio-economic realities. Nigerian initiatives to pursue financial restructuring, for instance, have been largely hamstrung due to civil and political unrest. Likewise, the government's insistence on micro-enterprises, instead of small and medium scale ventures, has done little to help Nigeria's burgeoning urban unemployed work force.

Another important consideration to this discourse is the difference between policy and implementation, which can at least partly be viewed as the difference between developed and developing nations worldwide. The best policies come to naught unless adequately executed, and the African continent provides a long list of such examples. Obasanjo's edict on entrepreneurial studies could very well end up being the next one unless successive governments follow it through in both letter and spirit. Nigeria needs to follow through on its significant economic potential with sincere governance and effective planning, together with an ironclad commitment to the fight against endemic corruption. Ill-planned interventionist policies and institutional mismanagement are potentially far more damaging in the long-term than, for example, the current economic crisis. A twofold agenda of reform and regulation, with effective implementation, is crucial to achieving the real entrepreneurial revolution that will help Nigeria finally overcome its troubled political and economic heritage.

Why Nigeria Needs to Focus on Entrepreneurial Development

In Nigeria, shaping *the future beyond oil* is a critical part of the national agenda. The current economy is dominated by the oil industry. The labour force of 47 million is growing, as is the unemployment rate, currently almost 20%, with many more millions of workers underemployed. Nigeria has the largest domestic market in Africa, a wide range of natural resources, and a diversely skilled labour pool. Given these economic realities, the country must constantly create new jobs, and diversify the industrial and commercial sectors to take advantage of human and natural resources.

Micro, small and medium enterprises (MSMEs) most of whom are located in the "informal" sector, provide a wide range of retail and service products for Nigeria's economy. Most MSMEs are small, sole proprietor or family businesses, largely "subsistence" in nature, that market their goods and services to urban and rural consumers. This is necessity entrepreneurship. There are also the "vibrant" larger scale entrepreneurial enterprises, employing non-family workers and constantly seeking opportunities to expand their operations. MSMEs provide the basis of economic survival for a major part of Nigeria's population.

As Nigeria pursues the National Economic Empowerment and Development Strategy (NEEDS), the Millennium Development Goals (MDGs), and Vision2020, a core part of the national strategy must be to grow and strengthen the vibrant elements of the MSME, largely informal, business sector. As a nation Nigeria must – cannot afford not to – invest in MSMEs. The country's economic future depends on it. It is noted that currently "at 69% of GNP, the country's informal economy is estimated to be one of the ten highest in the world, along with such countries as Georgia, Bolivia, Tanzania, Peru, and Azerbaijan." It is estimated that 90% of all new jobs created in the informal sector.

Much of the activity in the informal economy goes unreported. (Kazeem).

There are already existing governmental policies and activities which have helped spur entrepreneurship.   Elements of the SAP policy (1986), the National Directorate of Employment (NDE) and the establishment of industrial centres and the Small and Medium Enterprise Development Agency of Nigeria (SMEDAN) have all contributed to entrepreneurship and enterprise growth in Nigeria. SMEDAN sponsors and supervises entrepreneurship ventures while the Central Bank of Nigeria (CBN) provides financial support to entrepreneurs through the Small and Medium Enterprise Equity Investment Scheme (SMEEIS) of 2001. In addition, amendments to the indigenization decree in 1987 and the introduction of privatisation and commercialisation decrees in 1988, 1989 and 1995 boosted the development of indigenous entrepreneurship. Individual and group interest/awareness was aroused leading to venturing in mining, banking, knowledge industry, education, publishing, information technology etc. These and related policy initiatives have been of some help, but the full blown entrepreneurial revolution requires much greater policy facilitation.

Summary
The informal sector in Nigeria is a mammoth, heterogeneous operation that continues outside the purview of official regulation and monitoring. It encompasses a wide variety of unorganised and often unobserved small-scale activities that have traditionally sustained the country's urban and rural poor.

These activities can be classified into three broad categories:

1) Products: This sector comprises agricultural production, mining and quarrying, small-scale building and construction and machine-shop manufacturing. Traditional Nigerian crafts in clothing and furniture are other notable instances.

2) Services: This category includes a whole gamut of rural and urban services relating to education, health, counselling, labour, vehicle and mechanical repair, utility services, midwifery, etc.

3) Financial: Nigeria has numerous parallel finance structures operating mostly according to customary, unwritten rules. The most prominent example is Esusu, which offers loans by rotation from a contributory fund.

Although this is by no means an exhaustive definition, it does serve to highlight the extent and percolation of Nigeria's informal economy. It is not without reason that many observers have called it the backbone of the country's formal economy. If Nigeria is to get anywhere near the Millennium Development Goals by 2015, or its indigenous 2020 targets, a lot depends on its management of this tremendous unorganised powerhouse. The economic challenges facing Nigeria can be effectively and substantially reduced by transforming these subsistence activities into entrepreneurial ventures, this transformation serving as a vehicle for genuine and broad-based economic progress. For Nigeria, tapping into the informal economy requires more than just policy directives; it calls for an emphatic mind-shift in official and popular perception on the validity and inherent economic worth of activities that have colloquially been labelled as 'black market' enterprises.

Effective strategy has to involve an umbrella programme designed to provoke, sustain and enrich small businesses. Specifically, the Nigerian government has to deepen and widen the financial services availability to MSMEs, help develop sustainable markets for MSME products and services, and remove infrastructure and trade barriers that cripple their expansion. The informal economy has withstood the worst circumstances of historic and institutional neglect in Nigeria, and continues to flourish in the best traditions of entrepreneurial spirit despite tremendous local and international pressures.

The country's long-term macroeconomic performance is critically tied to its management of this sector, which can eventually prove much more valuable than its rich reserves of oil. Across the African continent in general and especially in Nigeria, the informal sector no longer plays an auxiliary role but leads official economies in terms of maintaining livelihoods and creating new jobs. Moreover, the needs to cultivate this sector and bring it under the tax regime if its long-term macroeconomic goals are to be achieved. The Nigerian informal economy is therefore critical on two counts: in terms of providing much needed internally generated revenue (IGR) and, more importantly, as the driving force behind rapid enterprise development for durable economic growth. In the effort to incorporate and develop the informal economy, Nigeria's government must:

- Devise innovative policy to bring unorganised activities under official regulation through a system of incentives, tax breaks and finance aimed at both existing and emerging unregulated businesses.
- Streamline tax and business regulations for universal applicability; crack down on systemic corruption through stringent penalties.
- Promote a credit environment sympathetic to small business realities. Lending should be at concessional rates.
- Improve productivity in small businesses through infrastructure development and removal of trade and administrative barriers. Strengthen technical support and capacity building assistance to existing and emerging entrepreneurs.
- Transform education at the vocational and skills level to create a dynamic manpower base that is equipped to meet entrepreneurial challenges; create supplementary programmes for relevant technology and computer education.

Sources

Antoine, Malick "Business Development Services, Unemployment and the Kenyan Informal Sector,"
http://fletcher.tufts.edu/research/2004/Antoine-Malick.pdf, accessed December 28, 2008

Appiah-Dolphyne, Nigeria's Banks, Stocks in Crises. *Daily Triumph*, 12 March 2009

ActionAid (2009) *Where Does It Hurt? The Impact of the Global Financial Crisis*. London, UK: ActionAid International.

ADB Statistics Department, Various domestic authorities and IMF *World Economic Outlook (March 2010)*.

Africa Economic Outlook, "Basic Indicators 2009"
http://www.africaneconomicoutlook.org/en/data-statistics/ accessed July 18, 2010

Africa Economic Outlook "Corruption Perception Index"
 http://www.africaneconomicoutlook.org/en/data-statistics/ accessed July 18, 2010

Central Bank of Nigeria (2008b) 'Remittances Data'. Trade and Exchange Office. Abuja, Nigeria: CBN.

Erumebor, Rume Wilson, "Globalization and the Nigerian Manufacturing Sector"
http://www.scribd.com/doc/32901345/Globalization-and-the-Nigerian-Manufacturing-Sector accessed July 20, 2010.

Fiaka, l., A. Adekoya, et al, "Nigeria: Global Financial Meltdown. Country Panics". *Vanguard*, 13 October, 2008

Global Research, "Nigerian Banks Collapse - Could Affect USA,"
September 4, 2009   http://www.globalresearch.ca/index.php?
context=va&aid=15058, accessed July 21, 2010.
Joseph, Richard A. *Democracy and Prebendal Politics in Nigeria:
the rise and fall of the Second Republic.* Ibadan, Nigeria : Spectrum
Books, c1991.

Kazeem, Ola. "Nigerian Economy: Is the Worst Over?"*In Defense of
Marxism* in Lagos Tuesday, 02 February 2010
http://www.marxist.com/nigerian-economy-is-worst-over.htm,
accessed on July 16, 2010.

King, David, "Nigeria Financial Sector Assessment", Report for
USAID / Nigeria, May 2003

Nigerian National Petroleum Corporation, "History Of The Nigerian
Petroleum Industry,"
http://www.nnpcgroup.com/history, accessed July 19, 2010.

Obadina, Tunde. "Myths about the Informal Economy," September
30, 2006, http://africatoday.eh7.co.uk/cgi-bin/public.cgi, accessed
December 28, 2008.

Obara, Lawyer C. and Ndukwe A. Ukpai, "Cost Accounting Practice
in the informal Sector of Nigeria : A Survey of Eastern Business
Zone," African Training and Research Centre in Administration for
Development, 2001, accessed December 28, 2008.

Soetan, Funmi "Technology and Women's Ventures in Nigeria's
Urban Informal Sector," http://www.idrc.ca/en/ev-30809-201-1-
DO_TOPIC.html, accessed December 28, 2008

United Nations, Department of Economic and Social Affairs,
Population Division, *World Population Prospects, 2008 Revision.*

United Nations Development Programme, *Human Development Report 2009 - HDI rankings* http://hdr.undp.org/en/statistics/ accessed July 18, 2010.

Vandenberg, Paul. Micro, Small and Medium-sized Enterprises and the Global Economic Crises, Impacts and Policy Responses (International Labour Organisation), 2009, http://www.ilo.org/public/libdoc/ilo/2009/109B09_80_engl.pdf, accessed July 10, 2010.

World Development Indicators database, World Bank, 1 July 2010 http://siteresources.worldbank.org/DATASTATISTICS/Resources/GDP.pdf, accessed July 18, 2010.

CHAPTER FOUR

ENTREPRENEURSHIP AND GLOBAL ECONOMIC RECOVERY FROM THE CRASH OF 2008

"There is nothing in life that we encounter that we are not equipped to handle. Tap into your talents and gifts and all of them will blossom."

Anonymous

Pursued correctly, entrepreneurship is lucrative and just. Today entrepreneurs have become one of the most dynamic economic forces in the world having a major impact on the global economy. This impact is felt even more deeply as the globalisation of business becomes even more widespread. Following up on the previous discussion focusing on Nigeria, this chapter discusses impacts of the current global economy crisis faced by the entrepreneurs worldwide. It looks at the effects of the global crisis on MSMEs, the challenges faced by entrepreneurs in developing countries, emerging economies, and developed countries, and the role and strategies of governments and the international community in encouraging entrepreneurship and global economic recovery.

Global Economic Meltdown

Analysts have identified various underlying causes of the global economic crisis which took hold in 2008. These causes include liberalisation of global financial regulations, boom and bust in the housing market, real estate speculation, new financial instruments, poor rating of risk, and high-risk loans, and government policies encouraging risky mortgage lending. (Adamu) The immediate trigger of the global crisis was the bursting of the United States housing bubble which peaked between 2005 and 2006 (Moyers; Lahart). Following the collapse in house prices, there was a major increase in default rates on sub-prime and adjustable rate mortgages (ARM).

An increase in loan packaging, marketing and incentives such as easy initial terms and a long-term trend of rising housing prices had encouraged borrowers to undertake difficult mortgages in the belief they would be able to quickly refinance at more favourable terms. Unfortunately, once interest rates began to rise and housing prices started to drop moderately in 2006-2007, refinancing became more difficult. Defaults and foreclosure activity increased dramatically as easy initial terms expired, home prices failed to rise as anticipated, and ARM rates reset even higher. Low interest rates and large inflow of foreign funds had created easy credit conditions for a few years before the crises, fuelling a housing construction boom and encouraging debt-financed consumption. The combination of easy credit and money inflows contributed to the United States housing bubble. Loans of various types were easy to get and consumers assumed an unprecedented debt load. As part of the housing and credit booms, the number of financial agreements such as mortgage-backed securities (MBS) and collateralised debt obligations (CDO), which derived their value from mortgage payments and housing prices, increased significantly. These financial innovations helped institutions and investors around the world to invest in the U.S. housing market. As the prices of housing started to decline, major global financial institutions that had borrowed and invested heavily in sub-prime MBS reported huge losses. Falling prices also resulted in homes worth less than the mortgage loan, providing a financial incentive to enter foreclosure. The ongoing foreclose epidemic that began in the late 2006 in the U.S. drained wealth from consumers and eroded the financial strength of banking institutions. Defaults and losses on other types of loans also increased significantly as the crisis expanded from the housing market to other parts of the economy. Global estimations of losses are in the trillions of U.S. dollars (IMF).

As the housing and credit bubbles built, a series of factors caused the financial system to both expand and become increasingly fragile, a process called *financialisation*. Policy makers did not recognise the increasingly important role played by financial institutions such as investment banks and hedge funds, also known as *shadow banking systems,* which some experts believe had become as important as commercial (depository) banks in providing credit. Regulated banks had also assumed significant debt burdens while providing the mortgage loans and did not have a financial cushion sufficient to absorb large loan defaults or MBS losses. These losses impacted the ability of financial institutions to lend and restore faith in the commercial paper markets which are important to funding business operations.

Another cause of the global crisis was the incorrect pricing of risk. Pricing of risk refers to the incremental compensation required by investors for taking additional risk, which could be measured by interest rates or fees. For different reasons, market participants did not measure the risk inherent with financial innovations accurately (innovations such as MBS and CDOs) or understand the impact of underpriced risk on the overall stability of the financial system. Massive and previously unthinkable losses dramatically impacted balance sheets across the globe, leaving them with little capital to continue operations.

This U.S. crisis rapidly spread into a global economic shock which lead to a number of European bank failures, major declines in various stock indexes, and large reductions in market value of equities and commodities. Both MBS and CDO had been purchased by corporate and institutional investors globally. And derivatives such as credit default swaps also increased the linkage between large financial institutions. Furthermore, the de-leveraging of financial institutions, as assets were sold to pay back obligations that could not be refinanced in credit markets, accelerated the insolvency crisis and caused a decrease in international trade.

Political leaders all over the world, national ministers of finance and central banks directors co-ordinated efforts to reduce fears, but the crisis continued. At the end of 2008 a currency crisis developed, with investors transferring vast capital resources into stronger currencies such as yen, the Dollar and the Swiss franc. Particularly hard-hit and vulnerable developed and emerging economies have sought emergency financial assistance from the International Monetary Fund (IMF).

Effects of the Economic Meltdown on Entrepreneurship

There have been multiple impacts of the global economic crisis on global entrepreneurial activity; these include:

Entrepreneurial Activity: Studies and analysis of the period July 2007 to 2008 have noted a drop of 8% in the rate of total entrepreneurial activity (TEA) in comparison with the previous year. The rate was measured before the recession had started to bite, which means that the impact of the crisis would have been fairly moderate.

Innovation: Analysts highlight the fact that innovation is the key for recovery in sectors like real estate, construction, and automobiles. Businesses invested less in latest generation technologies; capital investment fell from 10.6% in 2007 to 9.5% in 2008.

Size: The percentage of new businesses in 2008 employing between 1 and 5 people was, for the first time, greater than that of people who only created employment for themselves. 40.7% were self-employed and 41.7% contracted between 1 and 5 employees. 15% employed 6 and 19 employees and 2.6% had 20 or more employees.

Pullout Rates: The rates of abandonment of start-up or fledgling companies increased from 1% in 2007 to 1.3% in 2008, of which 0.97% were closures and 0.33% were sold to other firms.

Analysts estimate that between July 2007 and July 2008 more than 250,000 firms closed, and that this figure rose during the last quarter of 2008 due to the worsening macroeconomic scenario. (Global Entrepreneurship Monitor)

Studies have shown that during an economic recession fewer companies were founded and fewer successful companies emerge from that economically constrained population. This is so because entrepreneurs often delay creating companies until the economy in which they anticipate selling products or services is more robust. This applies most strongly to entrepreneurs in service industries where there is little lag time from company founding until first product/service sale. If there is a longer lag between company founding and product launch, we might not expect entrepreneurs, all things being equal, to hesitate as much in starting their new ventures because first revenues might be anticipated to more likely coincide with a resurgent economy. Other reasons why entrepreneurs may found fewer companies during the economic meltdown relates to their unwillingness to leave their current places of employment during a weak economy. And a more compelling obstacle is the limited availability of risk capital during the economic downturn, to the extent that it is difficult to raise money for a new entrepreneurial venture. There is also a demand issue. Even if similar numbers of companies are founded, it is plausible that more of these companies do not achieve material success due to the poor economy at founding, thus leading to poorer longer-term outcomes for cohorts of companies founded during weak economic periods.

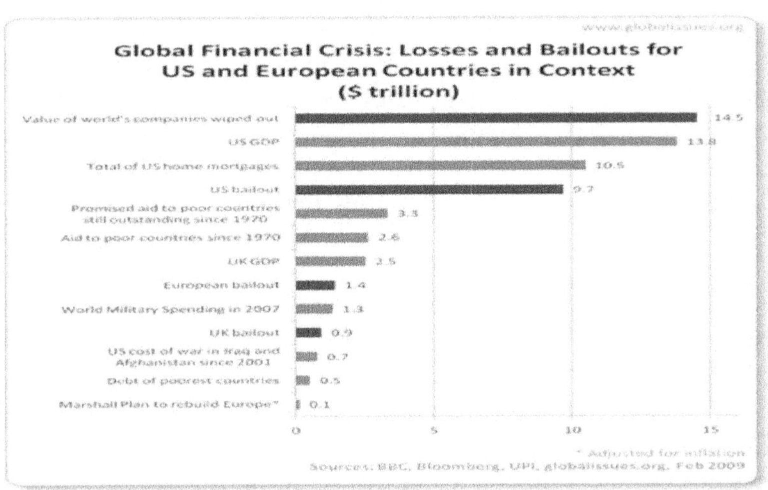

Challenges of Entrepreneurship in Developing Countries

There has been significant growth in developing countries as a group since 2001 due to the rapid increase in commodity prices which has in turn been growing due to the demand from emerging markets such as China, India and Brazil. In these countries growth has been export led. Countries with commodities that are still in demand over the long-term such as oil, will continue to grow. But the countries that will grow the fastest over the next few years will be those countries that have done the most during the past commodity and growth cycle to invest their gains in infrastructure and education and where the gains have been distributed is such a manner so that the middle class have been growing the most substantially. This will allow such countries the ability to better utilise domestic resources, including IGR tax revenues, to diversify their economies in the light of changes in the world economy.

Perhaps more than ever, countries with an evolving entrepreneurial economy will be able to achieve faster growth. These countries are committed to shaping conducive environments for the private sector to flourish, including political stability, strong property rights, and the rule of law. Corruption is a dominant obstacle to growth in many developing countries. Essentially, corruption entails a misallocation of entrepreneurial talent into activities that carry individual benefit, but has destructive or unproductive consequences for society at large.

Because of its predatory nature it reduces productive investments, leads to an outflow of talent, lowering growth rates and increasing income inequalities. Ideally, such talent should be re-allocated into productive activities. In many countries with poorly developed institutions, the existence of precious natural resources turn out to be a curse rather than a blessing, since these resources are 'lootable' and individuals and groups face little checks and balances in wanting to capture these for themselves. Nigeria provides an example of the misuse of revenues generated by its massive natural resource endowment.

Challenges of Entrepreneurship in Developed Countries

Developed countries are regarded as those that rank high in respect of a range of social and economic measure. One such measure is income per capita. Thus countries with high gross domestic product (GDP) per capita are described as developed countries. Another measure is industrialisation; countries in which the tertiary and quaternary sectors of the economy dominate are also classified as developed. Another measure recently considered is the Human Development Index, which combines national income, life expectancy and education measures. Developed countries rank high with regards to HDI. The developed countries have been adversely affected by the global crisis. As a group, their economic and financial policies and circumstances, while generally prudent, were not sufficiently robust to assure that they would be able to withstand the effects of the crisis. Some of these countries found it wise to turn to the IMF for precautionary stand-by arrangements, , that involve adjustments in economic and financial policies and related counter-cyclical measures, with the possibility of drawing on the Fund if their circumstances worsened.

Challenges of Entrepreneurship in Emerging Economies

A country is considered emerging because of its efforts to implement reforms and grow. An emerging economy meets two criteria. The first criterion is a rapid rate of economic growth and government policies that favour economic liberalisation; the second criterion is the adoption of a free-market system. Most of the emerging economies are located in central and Eastern Europe and Latin America. Some of the Central and Eastern European countries are Croatia, Hungary, Latvia, Romania, and Serbia. The Latin American countries are Argentina, Brazil, Chile, Uruguay, and Venezuela. Corruption is also of major concern within these countries.

While the consequences of the global economic crisis are not yet fully known, data and projections suggest that emerging economies were also affected, notably by more difficult international credit conditions and weaker demand from OECD countries. Calls for higher tariffs and more restrictive behind-the-border regulations have intensified. Litigation in the WTO has been on the increase.

Measures Taken to Address the Crisis

It is obvious that the developed and emerging economies will have to absorb and apply lessons learned about the supervision of financial and other markets in the aftermath of the crisis. Complementary measures across a range of economic policies will be required.

Reserve-Enhancing Measures: In light of the impact of the crisis on the availability of capital through the international markets, a number of countries have entered into swap arrangements so as to strengthen their reserve positions. A significant number of emerging markets have turned to the International Monetary Fund (IMF) for support. With the absence of a quick recovery in international credit markets, the IMF is likely to see increasing demand from emerging market countries facing declining exports and the need to roll-over substantial amounts of international debt.

Measures to Strengthen Financial Sectors: In many emerging economies measures have been taken to address the impact on the banking and the financial sector. For example, existing deposit insurance schemes have been modified to broaden the kinds of deposits covered or to increase the maximum covered. Capital injections directed at the banking sector and other support mechanisms for domestic banks, both to assist banks in meeting minimum capital injections and other adequacy standards and to support bank lending operations, especially in the critical area of trade credit. These measures mirror in large part those implemented to support domestic banking systems in the developed economies.

Fiscal Stimulus Packages: Some emerging economies have built up sizeable international reserves and run significant fiscal surpluses in recent years. These resources have supported stimulus packages involving, for example, government expenditure initiatives and temporary indirect tax reductions. Similar measures have been implemented in the OECD economies.

Protectionist Measures: The global crisis and the resulting domestic impacts, including sharply increased unemployment, have led to growing trade protectionism. Developed countries have instituted subsidies and other support packages. The emerging market countries have also been active, for example, in the automotive sector in protecting their component suppliers. Protectionist tendencies have also been evident in the financial sector: virtually all nations have focused their financial sector subsidies on domestically owned banks rather than subsidiaries of foreign banks.

Role of Entrepreneurship in Economic Recovery

The importance of entrepreneurship in economic recovery and development is very much the same in any economy. Entrepreneurial activity and the resultant financial gain are always beneficial to a nation. Entrepreneurship can especially help in the process of recovery from the economic crisis by generating employment. The global economic slump has been characterised by losses and layoffs at large firms as well as small and medium sized enterprises. The major pressures faced by these enterprises are reduced demand and lack of credit. Demand enhancing measures will assist all enterprises whilst access to finance needs more specific targeting for small firms.

Enterprise Development Initiatives

Stimulus measures intended to boost SME activities have been implemented by governments across the world. These measures include tax relief, increased credit availability, trade promotion, and limited assistance for informal and small enterprises. Small scale enterprise start-ups are likely to increase as laid-off workers try to make a living. Achieving success will be difficult for these SMEs due to the weak demand and limited access to credit. Banks are now risk averse, government oversight of their activities is far more stringent, and even good clients have difficulty securing credit. Governments, including those of the UK and India, are trying to reduce the credit shortfall by expanding loan guarantee programs for the SME sector.

Where possible, permanent layoffs are being avoided through various measures, such as work-time reductions, temporary shutdowns, training schemes and employee retention subsidies. The International Labour Organisation (ILO) has developed a Five Point Crisis Response to assist existing MSMEs to weather the economic downturn and support unemployed workers, including migrants, in creating self-employment. These five points focus on assessing environments and on providing advice, examples and training to policy makers, businesses and business associations.

These are:

Rapid assessments of the enterprise environment: The crisis has had a general impact on all economies around the world, but there are sectoral and geographical differences. The crisis has also hit economies and enterprises at different times and some will exit from the crises more rapidly and in better condition than others. A rapid assessment will pinpoint problem areas.

Advice through examples for policy makers on access to finance: Access to finance is a major constraint for MSMEs during the crisis. The ILO has produced this guide with considerable attention on the credit issue and provides a range of examples drawn from countries in various parts of the world. These examples offer ideas for policy makers and social partners in other countries on how to make a proactive approach to unblocking the financing constraint. However each country will need to work out its own approach based in its own set of banking institutions and credit programs, and on its resources, expertise and regulatory environment.

Advice to policy makers on public procurement: Several governments have responded to the economic crisis with demand stimulus measures that involve spending on public works. MSMEs in relevant sectors, notably road and building construction, can compensate for the decline in demand from private clients with increased servicing of public sector customers. Other micro or small businesses, not able to secure public contracts, can benefit by supplying or sub-contracting with other enterprises that have. The ILO has a training program on public procurement by MSMEs that can be used to provide advice and ideas to policy makers.

Advise and training on business development services: Small enterprises need to cope with reduced demand in their traditional markets and new opportunities arising during the crisis. Entrepreneurship is a complex issue involving personal attributes, a supporting culture and enabling policy environment. It can be assisted through training on how to start and mange a business. The ILO has promoted entrepreneurs through its Start and Improve Yourself Business (SIYB) suite. The ILO has also developed a network of 7,000 trainers and 277 licensed master trainers for the SIYB suite in over 500 partner organisations all over the world. With these the ILO can provide training for entrepreneurs and would be entrepreneurs on coping with reduced demand and seizing new opportunities.

Advice and training to strengthen enterprise associations:
Enterprise associations are a valuable support mechanism for businesses during an economic crisis. They allow members to share ideas and knowledge, provide information on new projects and programs and advocate on behalf of their member as well as governments. The effectiveness of such organisations varies considerably, depending on the ability to attract members, the level of funding and the leadership and management. The ILO strengthens these associations through its training program for small business associations so that these associations can play a more active role during the global economic downturn.

Summary

Developed, emerging and developing economies have all been impacted by the deep global recession. Equity markets have lost significant percentages of their value, many large financial and manufacturing companies have disappeared or been bailed out by their governments, unemployment has risen sharply, business and consumer credit has shrunk, commodity prices have experienced major declines, protectionist pressures have increased, and global demand has declined. Supporting the growth of SMEs or MSMEs has become a central part of policy initiatives of governments and international financial institutions and economic development organisations around the world. From the heart of the crisis in the U.S. to the margins of the global economy in Rwanda, government leaders are extolling the virtues of entrepreneurial development in terms of employment creation and economic diversification. These governments are extending current support and putting in place new encouragement for entrepreneurs, realising that for recovery to take place we "should start where most new jobs do – in small businesses, companies that begin when an entrepreneur takes a chance on a dream, or a worker decides it's time she became her own boss," (Obama) and for development to occur "it is essential to develop the private sector and to create an environment that enables entrepreneurs to flourish." (Kagame)

Sources

ActionAid (2009) *Where Does It Hurt? The Impact of the Global Financial Crisis.* London, UK: ActionAid International.

Adamu, Abdul, "The Effects of Global Financial Crisis on Nigerian Economy." Mimeo, Nasarawa State University, Keffi, Nasarawa State, Nigeria. April 30, 2009

"Financial Crisis of 2007-2010."
http://en.wikipedia.org/wiki/Financial_crisis_of_2007%E2%80%932
010 accessed July 10, 2010.

Gamberoni, Elisa and Richard Newfarmer, "Trade Protection:
Incipient but Worrisome Trends," Trade Notes, November, The
World Bank, March 2009.

Global Entrepreneurship Monitor (GEM) Report, January 29, 2009.
http://www.ie.edu/IE/php/en/noticia_.php?id=213 accessed July 10,
2010.

International Monetary Fund, "IMF Loss Estimates" (PDF) accessed
May 1, 2008.

Kagame, Paul, "The Backbone of a New Rwanda: Entrepreneurship
Is the Surest Way" *Innovations,* Winter 2010, Vol. 5, No. 1, Pages 3-
6 accessed July 23, 2010

Lahart, Justin (2007-12-24). 'Egg Cracks Differ in Housing, Finance
Shells' WSJ.com retrieved July 13, 2008.

Lander, Mark(2008-10-23). 'West Is in Talks on Credit to aid poorer
Nations'. The New York Times. Retrieved 2008-10-24

Molina, Nuria and Marta Ruiz, The cost of reserves: Developing
countries pay the price of global financial instability, January 2010.
http://www.eurodad.org/uploadedFiles/Whats_New/Reports/the_cost
s_of_reserves_lay_out.pdf accessed July 10, 2010.

Obama, Barack. *State of the Union Address.* 27 January, 2010

Vandenberg, Paul. Micro, Small and Medium-sized Enterprises and
the Global Economic Crises, Impacts and Policy Responses
(International Labour Organisation), 2009,

http://www.ilo.org/public/libdoc/ilo/2009/109B09_80_engl.pdf, accessed July 10, 2010.
"http://static.globalissues.org/i/economy/global-financial-crisis-bailout-in-context.png" * MERGEFORMATINET
Source: Global Issues, "Global Financial Crisis," http://www.globalissues.org/article/768/global-financial-crisis#Acrisissosoeveretheworldfinancialsystemisaffected, accessed August 1, 2010

CHAPTER FIVE

CHALLENGES AND OPPORTUNITIES FOR AFRICA'S ENTREPRENEURS

"Success is neither magical nor mysterious. Success is the natural consequences of consistently applying the basic fundamentals."

Jim Rohn

"The conditions will never be perfect for you. Just go ahead and on the way things will work themselves out."

Peter Osalor

The African Paradox

As of 2010 Africa's 54 different countries were inhabited by approximately 1 billion people. Africa is the poorest inhabited continent in the world. It is also the least developed as regards the quality of human development. Of the 182 countries ranked in the United Nations Development Programme Human Development Index for 2009, 22 African countries ranked among the 24 designated "low human development" nations of the world. (UNDP) The majority of Africa's people south of the Sahara live on less than the local equivalents of $2 per day.

Poverty head-count ratio at $1.25 a day (PPP) (% of population)

East Asia & Pacific	16.8%	2005
Europe & Central Asia	3.7%	2005
Latin America & Caribbean	8.2%	2005
Middle East & North Africa	3.6%	2005
South Asia	40.3%	2005
Sub-Saharan Africa	50.9%	2005

Poverty head-count ratio at $2 a day (PPP) (% of population)

East Asia & Pacific	38.7%	2005
Europe & Central Asia	8.9%	2005
Latin America & Caribbean	17.1%	2005
Middle East & North Africa	16.9%	2005
South Asia	73.9%	2005
Sub-Saharan Africa	72.9%	2005

Source: World Bank, Data: Poverty Headcount Ratios
http://data.worldbank.org/topic/poverty

Poverty is widespread. Diseases and its high incidence rates are directly linked to high poverty levels (HIV/AIDS, tuberculosis, malaria, tuberculosis, measles), are endemic. Illiteracy is also higher in sub-Saharan Africa than in any other world region. This state of affairs is a result of the continent's colonial underdevelopment, post-independence, internal political struggles and instability aggravated by the global cold war conflict, widespread corruption and despotism, and inappropriate and inconsistent macroeconomic policies.

The picture is not all bleak. Since 2000 the African economy has grown at a faster rate (an average of 4.9%) than those of Latin America and Central and Eastern Europe. Even though the global crisis slowed it did not halt GDP growth: in 2008 the African economy grew 2%, in 2009 2.5%, and it is estimated to grow almost 5% in 2010. (African Economic Outlook) This is heartening news, and makes it clear that Africa is potentially a vibrant, dynamic part of the global economy. Over a decade ago, at the beginning of Africa's growth spurt Kofi Annan had pointed out that "Africa's profitability is one of the best-kept secrets in today's world economy." There is increasing recognition that Africa offers profitable opportunities for investors and entrepreneurs.

The "African Lions" – Algeria, Botswana, Egypt, Libya, Mauritius, Morocco, South Africa, and Tunisia – are the strongest African economies. (Aquila) Of course, there are significant differences in terms of the economic fortunes of African states. World Bank 2009 estimates for GDP per capita in Africa range from $31,837 in Equatorial Guinea to $320 in the Democratic Republic of the Congo. The African continent contains the diversified, industrialised economy of South Africa and the marginal, conflict ridden, pirate economy of Somalia. It is also the case that much of the GDP growth experienced in Africa since 2000 has been driven in significant part due to robust demand for oil and minerals. For example, the price of oil reached unprecedented levels in the first half of 2008. China's demand for a wide range of minerals has driven metal prices higher, including those of Zambian copper and South African gold. (OECD) Foreign investment from China and India have helped spur Africa's growth. It is estimated that China's trade with Africa totalled US$100 billion in 2008, a tenfold increase from 2001.

However, Africa's growth is also being driven by growing African entrepreneurship, which is recognised as a "crucial ingredient of African success." (Aquila)

Matthew Ashimolowo points out in his book *What is Wrong with Being Black?* that Africa is replete with natural resources that should be the basis of a wealthy continent. In addition to Nigeria, mineral-rich African nations include:

- The Democratic Republic of Congo has over a million metric tons cobalt metal.

- Morocco has a similar cobalt metal

- Beryllium is found in Madagascar, Mozambique, the Democratic Republic of Congo, and Zimbabwe.

- Chromium is found in the whole of South Africa and parts of West Africa.

- Manganese is found in most of West Africa as well as in the Kalahari Desert.

- Gabon has oil fields and vanadium; a rare element used to make steel tougher and to make steel shock resistant.

-

- Nigeria has not just oil fields or oil wells. Nigeria has 32 trillion tons of natural gas. It has been burning away for the past 30 years and the deposit still remains at 32 trillion. Nigeria also has titanium, and a metallic element tanatlom, a metallic element resembling titanium.

- Lithium is found in large deposits in the Democratic Republic of Congo and Rwanda. This is used in some cases to make mobile phones.

- Platinum deposits are found in South Africa.

- The Democratic Republic of Congo is the world's chief source of radium.

- Uranium is found in the Democratic Republic of Congo, but the largest deposit of uranium is found in Niger just above Nigeria.

- Most of Africa's copper is found in Central Africa, particularly Zambia, Malawi, Central Africa Republic. Zambia has 36 million tons. The Democratic Republic of Congo has 26 million tons of copper. Botswana, a very small country, has 530,000 tons of copper metal reserves. Mauritania has the largest reserve of copper in West Africa, 740,000 tons. Uganda has 200,000 tons of copper.

- The whole of Africa has a billion tons of lead reserve. North Africa, though, is the largest producing region.

- Zinc deposit in Africa is 16.5 million tons. Morocco and Algeria have large deposits of Zinc.

- Phosphate is found in large deposits in North Africa, the Democratic Republic of Congo, and some parts of Nigeria.

Morocco and Western Sahara have large deposit of phosphate to the tune of 20,000 billion tons. The regions of Western Sahara, Algeria, Tunisia all together have 12,000 billion tons of phosphate. Egypt has 660 million tons of phosphate. Togo has 60 million tons of phosphate.

- Senegal has 140 million tons of phosphate. The world's only source of aluminium phosphate is found in Senegal. It is estimated to be one hundred million tons.

- Other phosphate deposits are found in Tanzania, 10 million tons. Uganda 180 million tons. Malawi 18 million tons.

- Granite is found in Morocco and Nigeria. Nigeria's granite being of particular interest, the only unique, sandy-looking granite in the world. Vast reserves of granite are found in Burkina Faso.

- Quartzite is found in Uganda and the Democratic Republic of Congo.

- Dolerite is produced in South Africa.

- Marble is found in Nigeria, Mali, Togo, and South Africa.

- Limestone is a key element in the production of cement, worldwide and it is found in large deposits in West Africa. It goes from West Africa across to Central Africa, down to the Atlantic coasts, with major deposits of it in Togo, Ghana, East Africa countries like Kenya, Tanzania, Uganda, Zambia, and South Africa.

- North Africa has a major reserve of Jepson on the Mediterranean coast. This also is used in building. Somalia has a reserve of 30 million tons of Jepson.

- Nigeria has an unquantified deposit of bitumen. There is so much that it is taking over farmlands and yet the country imports bitumen.

- Major metallic deposits are also found all across Africa.

- In Algeria, iron ore is said to be 1.5 billion metric tons. This is also found in Western Mauritania.

- In Mauritania there is 27 million tons of copper ore. Manganese is also found in Algeria.

- In Algeria in particular, various metallic deposits that are necessary for different works are found. This list includes tin, nickel, chromium, zinc, lead, cobalt, silver, gold, platinum, and molybdenum, a metallic element used in strengthening steel. Wolfram is used as a source of tungsten in electricity; thorium, a radioactive metallic element; and uranium.

The African paradox, similar in many ways to the Nigerian paradox, is that despite the continent's wealth in natural resources, mass poverty, and the resultant social unrest are widely prevalent. For many countries, population growth has matched or outpaced GDP growth meaning that average incomes have remained stagnant. Thus, even though the continent's GDP has grown, the global recession means that it is even more unlikely that African countries will achieve the Millennium Development Goal of halving the number of people living in poverty by 2015. (African Economic Outlook) The other MDGs are also in jeopardy of being missed.

Sectors of the African economy

Agriculture: About 60% of the African workers are employed by the agricultural sector, three-fifths being subsistence farmers. Subsistence farming unfortunately, fails to produce enough to make re-investment possible. Large scale farming is normally operated by large corporations and covers tens of square kilometres and employs a large number of labourers. These farms produce cash crops such as coffee, cocoa, cotton and rubber.

In West Africa, agriculture accounts for an estimated 40% of combined GDP and employs up to 70% of the available working population. Agricultural commodities are the second largest export from the region to the European Union, although most goods are traded without any local value addition. This represents a significant failure to produce high-value products that can enhance profitability in agro-operations and provide much-needed employment.

Africa's farmers also compete in domestic and international markets against European and North American farmers who are heavily subsidised by their governments. African agricultural exports are also hindered by non-tariff barriers such as the need to comply with international production standards. Further, the region's high transportation costs inflate the price of agro-products in local markets and lower export competitiveness. The gross outcome of these conditions is that developing economies in West Africa and elsewhere generate only $40 by processing one ton of agricultural products against $180 in developed countries. The generally low productivity in Africa's agricultural sector is due to a range of interrelated factors. These include:

- Inadequate rural infrastructure and agricultural services
- Low levels of education of farmers
- Under-investment in agricultural research
- Low application of fertiliser

- Slow adoption of high yielding crop varieties
- Lack of access to small-scale irrigation and credit
- Limited opportunities for trade in domestic and international markets for agricultural products.
(African Development Bank)

Mining and Drilling: Africa is rich in minerals and petroleum and a few countries possess and export the vast majority of these resources. The southern nations have large reserves of diamonds, gold and copper while petroleum is concentrated in Nigeria, its neighbouring states, and Libya. FDI in Africa is largely linked to the exploitation of this wealth of natural resources. Although oil and minerals yield most of Africa's revenues, the industry employs only about two million people. Profits from the exploitation of these resources go to government or large corporations and both have been known to squander this money on luxuries for the elite or on mega-projects that return little value.

Manufacturing: Africa is the least industrialised continent in the world. Only about 15% of Africa's workforce is employed in the industrial sector. Only a handful of countries - Egypt, South Africa, Tunisia and Morocco - have substantial manufacturing sectors. Nearly all of the continent's natural resources are exported for secondary refining and manufacturing. Africa's abundant natural resources provide the basis for an industrial revolution as an integral part of an entrepreneurial revolution. Education, adequate infrastructure and stable electricity are key to attracting domestic and foreign investment.

Investment banking: Banking in Africa has been problematic because local banks are often unstable; governments and industry rely largely on international banks. In recent years banking reform has been of major priority for the IMF and World Bank. One important reform achieved was obtaining permission for increased penetration by foreign banks.

Egypt and South Africa are the most successful nations in attracting local operation of foreign banks.

Communication and Information technology: Africa has the highest growth rate of cellular subscribers in the world, with markets growing twice as fast as the Asian Markets. This has even contributed to the creation of a base for cellular banking. Countries like Namibia and Kenya have attracted attention with new phone services and by liberalising regulatory controls are producing a boom in internet services demand.

Corruption and Greed in Africa

Widespread corruption continues to be a major impediment to economic growth in Africa. The existence of corrupt systems of government and unethical business practices in Africa as a whole is indisputable. The source of such corruption and greed is a debated subject. Did the culture of corruption evolve from African traditions, such as bearing gifts to a king in order for protection for your family, or did most of today's corrupt ideas result from actions of imperialists, hungry for profits at any human cost?   Whatever
the source of corruption in Nigeria and the rest of Africa, much of the ill-gotten gains has been deposited in Western banks. Corrupt payments, passed through secretive trust funds in British offshore islands or Swiss accounts, are rarely met with question. From these accounts the funds are often funnelled into London, or other Western cities, perhaps explaining why corruption perpetuates and Western governments seem to avoid investigation.

Although the original source of Africa's business and political corruption cannot be ascribed to one period in history, there are significant factors which have fuelled a culture of corruption.

These factors include (but are not limited to) promotion of ethic competition, money changing and currency depreciation schemes, and modern technology.

Technology and Current Scams, Tricks, and Illegal Business

Though global technology, such as the Internet and mobile phones, has provided great opportunities to a largely undeveloped Africa, it has also opened wide the door of opportunity for illegitimate business worldwide. Nigeria, of all the African countries, holds one of the worst reputations for scams, tricks, and unethical methods of stealing money–and with the advent of e-mail, a reputation that has gone global.

Whether it's an email stating that the recipient will earn a large sum of money for helping a poor Nigerian family transfer their inheritance or a business wholesale request to pay with credit card, the e-mail scams originating from Nigeria are numerous numbering in the thousands. Moreover, hackers and scammers in other countries have begun to mimic Nigerian scams, taking them technologically to new levels of sophistication, and even under the pretence that they too, are Nigerian.

Taking Advantage of the Oil Industry: Corruption Begets Corruption

As the majority of Nigerians witness the daily corruption in business that keeps the wealthy extremely rich and powerful, some have taken on their own corrupt measures in order to make gains from the industry. The Niger Delta has enshrined a reputation for banditry and lawlessness. For example, some farmers and landowners have been accused of purposely cutting the oil pipes near their homes to create a spill. These poor farmers and villagers can then claim compensation–a corrupt enterprise that is more profitable than farming, say the oil companies. The Oil companies, long viewed as greedy and uninterested in advancing the welfare of local life, continue to be the target of corrupt and even violent schemes. Theft of oil resources called "bunkering" causes Shell to report a loss of up to 100,000 barrels of Nigerian crude oil per day (Dowden). The economic, political and environmental impacts are great; the stolen oil funds local militias and keeps Nigeria at the edge of war, and the damaged wetlands and forests that are a blight on the landscape and destroy locally sustainable Micro and Small industries Environmentally, the Niger Delta gas flares are among the biggest single contributors to global warming. Villages that literally sit on top of large oil reserves remain destitute, and its inhabitants unemployed by the large international companies pumping black gold out from under their feet.

While entrepreneurs and large companies alike are moving to diversify Nigeria's economy to include other resources such as natural gas, others fear that the country will only switch dependence from one raw material to another. Or, other illicit trade industries–such as the international black market drug trade, for which Nigeria is a well-known hub–will begin to rise to even greater prominence than they are currently.

As discussed previously, the first oil well was drilled in Nigeria in the mid-twentieth century. In 1956, a 12,000-foot well was dug at Olubiri, and the story unfolded in a plot similar to the tale of King Midas.
Nigeria was suddenly rich. The African country with the most people was blessed with an endless cheap source of energy and wealth. But it turned Nigeria into a nation of junkies. The sweet black juice oozed everywhere, into everything, It suffocated the economy, generated greed, fed regional jealousy, funded terrible regimes, started a war. Oil dreams wrecked Nigeria, and Olubiri was where they all began (Dowden).

Although the amazing resource attracted large companies such as Shell, Exxon Mobil, Texaco, Agip, and Elf, among others, today there is only one gas station in the entire surrounding province where the oil was struck.

To the villagers, their richest resource is unobtainable. According to one village Chief, the effects of the oil industry have set Nigerians back:

> We were expecting to be living in paradise. We thought we had the only oil on the Niger Delta. But to this day we have never benefited from Shell. They have built no project here. And now the river is polluted with oil spills and there are fewer and fewer fish. We grow food but the black smoke from the oil fires forms on the leaves. There used to be 8000 people in this village, now there are less than 6000....the only development in this village is a bit of road we have made ourselves by hand, but it takes us two days to get to market. Most of the trade we do now is barter with the next village, fish for yams. (Africa).

In addition to the lack of prosperity for Africans, the lack of diversification leaves the economy of Nigeria at the mercy of the oil industry, dangerously lacking stability and promising to keep the current system in government in place for many years. With the early promise of riches, the discovery of oil toppled nearly every other industry in Nigeria that had existed before the twentieth century. In the later half of the twentieth century, only about 3% of government revenue streamed in from sources other than oil, proving that the economy of Nigeria was totally controlled by crude oil and the companies behind it. Today, oil accounts for about 30% of Nigeria's Gross Domestic Product. The country is currently the world's eighth largest crude producer with known reserves in excess of 36 billion barrels. Despite this resource base, Nigeria is forced to import almost 85% of domestic fuel needs largely due to mismanagement of its four state-owned refineries. Together with vandalism and violence in the Niger Delta, this has led to huge production shortfalls that cost the country over $16 billion between 2005 and 2007 alone. The losses amount to an estimated 20% of Nigeria's combined production capacity of 2.5 million barrels per day. Moreover, the government has to pay oil companies the difference between import costs and the regulated retail price to make oil more affordable locally. Since 2005, the Nigerian government has sought to curb oil imports by offering exploration and production incentives to companies involved in oil refining and power generation. However, even though more than 20 private refinery licenses have been issued since, not a single project has taken off so far. Further, plans to privatise state-held oil refining operations have been on hold for several years, largely due to heavy subsidies in fuel prices that makes local refining unviable. Conflict, corruption and lack of official transparency have together caused several major foreign investments to be delayed or altogether aborted.

Although there is limited data on the subject, Nigeria's oil industry in its present state represent huge losses in terms of potential employment generation and enterprise development. Most existing exploration, production and refining operations run exclusively on raw material and technical imports, with no backward linkages to the local economy. Further, a relatively low standard of education means that technical jobs have almost always to be filled by foreign workers.

While much government effort in recent years has been devoted to reversing the country's traditional dependence on non-renewable mineral resources, the oil and gas industry is predicted to grow exponentially over the next few years. With oil accounting for 81% of present government revenue, the Nigerian National Petroleum Corporation (NNPC) has a major role to play in reversing decades of economic stagnation and driving massive entrepreneurial growth.

Despite its chequered past, the company has been responsible for significant achievements in Nigeria's economic development:

- NNPC oversaw the country's first equity stake in oil production with the Agip Oil Company in the mid-60s to better exploit resources for national development.

- It spearheaded oil exploration to confirm Nigeria's position as the top crude exporter in Africa in the 1970s, boosting oil revenue from N200 million to N10 billion through the decade.

- In 2004, the NNPC unveiled plans to launch the ambitious West African Gas Pipeline to supply Nigerian natural gas to several neighbouring countries.

- Nigeria emerged as an important exporter of natural gas with the establishment of the liquefied natural gas plant in Bonny in 2005 as part of efforts to end gas flaring by the end of this year.

- NNPC entered into a $1 billion joint-venture in the offshore Agbami fields to increase national crude production capacity by a further 250,000 barrels per day.

- Through its recent Okapi Power Plant, the NNPC will generate the first carbon credit in compliance with the Kyoto Protocol and related UN resolutions.

The reality is that it is oil revenue that funds Nigerian government initiatives to diversify the economy and achieve rapid enterprise revolution across non-oil sectors. Optimising the performance of the oil and gas sector of Nigeria's economy over the next decade to provide the financial backing for an entrepreneurial revolution will involve:

- Enhancing access to capital and technology and promoting independent control of joint-venture investments.

- Multiplying gas production and improving transmission to both domestic and regional gas markets.

- Establishing strategic partnerships with global gas companies to secure presence in international markets.

- Achieving production efficiency and selective growth to improve capacity in joint-venture operations.
- Rationalising the NNPC portfolio to ensure focus on high-growth potential assets.

- Extending refineries and gas-based industries to help turn Nigeria into a regional hub for petroleum products.

- Reducing operational constraints and production suspensions resulting out of vandalism and violence.

- Implementing further reforms in the oil and gas sector to improve transparency and boost investor confidence.

- Deregulating oil prices to reduce fiscal burden on the government and to promote private sector investment in refining operations.

- Enhancing equity finance access to emerging oil refining companies; sops and financial incentives to attract foreign direct investment.

- Improving capacity utilisation in existing refineries by raising production standards to cut dependence on finished petroleum imports.

- Diversifying the fuel retail business by deregulating the downstream sector and encouraging business expansion of existing players.

- Enforcing environmental compliance and addressing genuine concerns of local communities; increasing social participation and minimising conflicts.

Nigeria's extensive resource base and human capital make it ideal for an enterprise revolution that drives explosive growth and creates a closely-inter-linked entrepreneurial economy.

Nigeria's recent attempts to drive SME growth in the non-oil sector are commendable; however, these efforts do not take away the imperative of further development and optimisation of its flagship industry. Only after achieving self reliance in oil can Nigeria hope to develop a thriving and diversified economy.

Pursuing Economic Development

As made clear from the preceding analysis, governments and civil societies in Nigeria and across Africa must work together to build a partnership that creates an environment that empowers workers and entrepreneurs, and uses training and technology to drive productivity increases. The rapid growth of China and India has lifted millions out of poverty. In contrast, much of Africa is growing too slowly to increase significantly GDP per capita. African countries need to channel resources from recent growth into public policy initiatives to address the pressing issues of poverty, youth unemployment and rapid urbanisation. (Patteron & Marzo) Key priorities for Africa are infra-structural development (upgraded roads and electricity networks, improved access to water and sanitation) and development of the private sector. SME growth is evident on the African continent, but much more needs to be done. In order to tackle Africa's mass poverty, policies and programmes must be put in place to upgrade the knowledge and skills of workers, and, thereby, enhance competitiveness, increase productivity and real incomes. (African Development Bank) As part of the effort to develop the private sector, entrepreneurship training initiatives must be implemented to encourage self-employment. Post-training micro loans must also be available to jump-start enterprise development, and facilitate the incorporation of Africa's informal sector into the mainstream global economy. (African Economic Outlook)

In order for the whole of Africa to use entrepreneurship and trade as a platform for development and poverty eradication, some policies and programmes need to be put in place. The following are some policies that can enhance entrepreneurship in Africa:

Lowering the overall cost of doing business by reducing bureaucratic red tape. In most African countries, there are many bureaucratic practices that stifle the process of setting up and maintaining a business. This red tape discourages entrepreneurs from investing. To combat this, some countries have already established a single business license.

- Improvement of infrastructure is necessary in creating an environment that favours business practices. Factors such as power, road network, security and others can influence whether trade can thrive or not. Without proper infrastructure, both foreign and local investment is greatly hampered.

- Varied sources of venture capital to finance business start-ups and to assist in expanding already existing businesses must abound. In addition, mentorship organisations should be established in both rural and urban areas.

- The political will has to exist to ensure that policies and legislation's related to trade are pushed to the forefront to ensure that they are implemented. The political class needs to take leadership in this effort because they are the ones with the authority to make the right decisions.

In the remaining three chapters, the discussion focuses on:

1) Elaborating in greater detail the steps that governments must take to build the business environment that will allow the entrepreneurial revolution to take place.

2) The opportunities that exist in Nigeria and throughout Africa to grow and diversify economies by means of enterprise development.

3) How individuals can seize the many opportunities to realise their potential and shape their destinies by participating in the entrepreneurial revolution.

Sources

African Development Bank/African Development Fund, "Bank Group Policy on Poverty Reduction," February, 2004
http://www.afdb.org/fileadmin/uploads/afdb/Documents/Policy-Documents/10000028-EN-BANK-GROUP-POLICY-ON-POVERTY-REDUCTION.PDF

African Economic Outlook, "AfDB/OECD/UNECA report forecast Africa's growth to rebound in 2010,"24/05/2010
http://www.africaneconomicoutlook.org/en/news-events/article/afdb-oecd-uneca-report-forecast-africas-growth-to-rebound-in-2010-56/, accessed August 13, 2010.

Aquila, Frank, "Africa's Biggest Score: A Thriving Economy"
Bloomberg Businessweek
http://www.businessweek.com/investor/content/jun2010/pi20100628
_516449.htm, accessed August 9, 2010

Ashimolowo, Matthew, *What's Wrong with Being Black?*
Shippensburg, PA.: Destiny Image Publishers, Inc., 2007.

Dowden, Richard. *Africa: Altered States, Ordinary Miracles*. New
York: Perseus Books, Public Affairs, 2009.

 OECD, "Africa's economy: Aid and growth," OECD Observer No
249, May 2005
http://www.oecdobserver.org/news/fullstory.php/aid/1618/Africa_92s
_economy:_Aid_and_growth_.html, accessed August 2, 2010

Pattrerson, Sala and Federica Marzo "An Overview of the African
Economy" OECD Observer No. 279, May 2010
http://www.oecdobserver.org/news/fullstory.php/aid/3255/Africa_92s
_outlook.html, accessed August 2, 2010
Oruwari, Yomi. Youth in Urban Violence in Nigeria: A Case Study of
Urban Gangs from Port Harcourt, Working Paper No. 14.
http://core.geog.berkeley.edu/ProjectsResources/ND
%20Website/NigerDelta/WP/14-Oruwari.pdf accessed July 12,
2010.

Small Business Entrepreneur Blog, "Entrepreneurs Thrive During
Hard Times, According to Babson/Baruch U.S. GEM Report, Posted
on 28 November 2009,
http://www.energybyte.com/blog/entrepreneurs-thrive-during-hard-
times-according-to-babsonbaruch-u-s-gem-report accessed July 10,
2010.

United Nations Development Programme, *Human Development
Report 2009 - HDI rankings* http://hdr.undp.org/en/statistics/

accessed July 18, 2010.

Vandenberg, Paul. Micro, Small and Medium-sized Enterprises and the Global Economic Crises, Impacts and Policy Responses (International Labour Organisation), 2009, http://www.ilo.org/public/libdoc/ilo/2009/109B09_80_engl.pdf accessed July 10, 2010.

CHAPTER SIX

THE ENTREPRENEURIAL REVOLUTION: THE WAY FORWARD FOR NIGERIA

"[those who] bring the new technologies and the new concepts into active commercial use. They are the change agents of capitalism."

Lester Thurow

For Nigeria's and Africa's women, youth, rural populations, the urban poor, the underemployed and unemployed, the current economic realities offer no hope for a change in their circumstances. Mass poverty is endemic across the continent, and shows no signs of waning. Most of Africa's 54 countries are consistently listed among the low and low-medium human development societies. What is required to transform this situation is a radical break from the past. What is required is an entrepreneurial revolution devoted to providing goods and services that take advantage of the large domestic and regional markets and the opportunities of a globalised economy. But this will not happen by wishful thinking. It requires a profound shift in individual mindsets and a fundamental reorganisation of government policies and practices.

It will not happen overnight; but it can happen. Pursuing such a revolution, practical, directed steps can be taken immediately to encourage the entrepreneurial vision, talents and efforts of Nigeria's, and Africa's, populations. The entrepreneurial revolution is key to poverty alleviation. Such a revolution holds out realistic hope for the future of Africa's 1 billion people. This chapter elaborates on the substance of and critical need for an entrepreneurial revolution in Nigeria. It pays close attention to the challenges of employment generation and economic diversification, makes the case for the concerted effort to grow the MSME sector, and spells out the need for creating an environment conducive to entrepreneurship.

In the opening discussion of this book, U.S. President Obama and Rwandan President Paul Kagame highlight the crucial role of entrepreneurialism for economic recovery, transformation and development. For Obama "the true engine of job creation in this country will always be America's businesses. But government can create the conditions necessary for businesses to expand and hire more workers."(Obama).

For Kagame, building an entrepreneurial society is crucial as Rwanda recovers from past conflicts and grows its future, he declares:

> It is increasingly clear to us that entrepreneurship is the surest way for a nation to meet those goals and to develop prosperity for the greatest number of people. In fact, government activities should focus on supporting entrepreneurship not just to meet these measurable targets, but to unlock people's minds, to allow innovation to take place, and to enable people to exercise their talents. In all people, you find different kinds of talents, and entrepreneurship is about harnessing those talents and making sure that it takes people to another level in their personal development. So, for us in government, it is essential to develop the private sector and to create an environment that enables entrepreneurs to flourish. We have much more to do, and it will take time. We are focused on lowering the costs of electricity, providing access to finance, building roads, and training managers.

> Change has to start in the mind. And that is what we have been working on over time. Once the mind gets correct, the rest becomes simple.

> The Rwandese entrepreneurial mindset must be characterised by ambition, moral purpose, respect, openness to new ideas, and self-determination. This entrepreneurial mindset must I nform our actions whether we are in the private sector, government, or civil society. This mindset must inspire our entrepreneurs to aim ever higher. It must compel our civil servants to reinvent government. It must encourage our civil society to work for the greater good. Ultimately, this mindset holds the key to our prosperity, our development, and our future.

The two presidents make clear the significance of an entrepreneurial revolution. One, for the world's largest economy and for one of the world's smallest. These national leaders place emphasis on both the roles of individual entrepreneurs in innovation, job creation, and economic growth, and the responsibilities of governments in creating the conditions for entrepreneurial activity. Entrepreneurs and governments working together in public-private partnerships to pursue economic opportunities is the essence of the entrepreneurial revolution.

The Entrepreneurial Revolution Defined

The entrepreneurial revolution is best defined as a radical and co-ordinated attempt to accelerate wealth creation through the promotion of innovative business practices. The objective of this revolution is rapid and sustainable economic expansion with a specific focus on unique and creatively-evolved business models. It is a radical and co-ordinated attempt to accelerate wealth creation through the promotion of innovative business practices. It is also a point of convergence when and where a great number of entrepreneurs will put into motion an irreversible chain reaction of productive ventures outside the limits of cynicism and fear. It is this entrepreneurial spirit that is empowering countries like China, India along with Russia and the former Soviet satellite countries in Eastern Europe and the Baltic States, to rise above the gravity of years of under-employment, and centralised control of the economy.

The entrepreneurs in these countries are creating new wealth and generating income-yielding opportunities for so many with their vision, their daring, their sense of innovation and their passion for results. Even in United States which has been the world's leading economic power for so long, the new creators of wealth are the young entrepreneurs in the realm of information technology. There is a valuable lesson here that we should never miss. The most effective

way to get closer to the threshold of prosperity and to be removed farther from the weight of poverty is through an entrepreneurial revolution. As true of any successful revolution, no radical change happens overnight. No society can leapfrog from a stage of being a mere supplier of raw materials to one capable of orchestrating great tasks and events. There are no short-cuts.
To develop a nation of entrepreneurs, there must be a multi-sectoral, multi-level and multi-phase undertaking that begins with a collective resolve to break out of the old mould of doing things. The business community should spearhead an Entrepreneurial Revolution that makes a winner of everybody.

The entrepreneur in his entrepreneurial activities can bring about increase in production, create employment, income, and facilitate rapid growth of micro, small, medium, and large scale enterprises to reduce poverty and hunger among the people. Entrepreneurship is a very important element of economic growth. Entrepreneurship could be referred to as the ability of a nation's citizens, and of foreign investors, to engage in building new businesses, or in restructuring existing establishments in order to adjust to changes in the economic and political environment.

Entrepreneurship, in turn, may be facilitated by economic growth. Economists from Schumpeter to Rostow have argued that the enterprising aspect of entrepreneurship is vital for economic advancement and growth. Entrepreneurship leads to greater productivity, and hence economic growth. Top world economies – across Europe, the Americas and Asia – owe their prosperity in large part to the emergence of strong entrepreneurial movements that optimally leveraged available natural and human resource capitals. Today, the same economies are once again banking heavily on enterprise development to bail them out of the present economic downturn. History provides strong evidence of the utility of the entrepreneurship path to economic growth. Former British Prime Minister Margaret Thatcher holds the distinction of pioneering the first entrepreneurial revolution of its kind in an effort to overcome the recession that hit UK in the early 1980s. The 'Iron Lady' pushed through an intensive reforms process, taming labour unions and privatising under-performing public sector ventures, as a means of jump-starting a flagging economy. Specifically, the strategic focus on promoting private enterprises paid off more than expected and Britain's incredible resurgence set off a world-trend in economic growth. The controversial, though successful, policies of the Thatcher era soon became a benchmark that was enthusiastically adopted by developed and developing economies across the world.

Breaking the Nigerian Poverty Cycle through Entrepreneurial Revolution

One of many countries to remain untouched by the wave of economic affluence emanating out of Britain was its former West African colony – Nigeria. A troubled past marked by extended conflict and misrule has left the country in a curious situation that economists commonly refer to as the Nigerian paradox: a continuing condition of widespread poverty and underdevelopment despite the abundance of natural and human resources and fertile land. The paradox is due in part to the over dependence on oil and gas exports, and the lack of economic diversification. There are, however, other profound underlying causes.

These include:

- Articulate, but incompletely executed development plans

- Inconsistent, contradictory macro-economic policies

- Policy implementation designed to promote narrow self-interests rather than the national interest

- Limited government transparency and accountability

- Political instability and cultural divisions

- Massively skewed income distribution

- A consuming, unproductive society

- Poor management and exploitation of natural resources

- Limited investment in human capital development

- A reward system based on political contacts rather than competence and innovation

- Pervasive public sector corruption

- A law and order crisis, with constant threats to personal and property security

- Near collapse of social and economic infrastructure

- High macroeconomic volatility

- Poor financial management at all levels of government

- Rapid urbanisation

- Increasingly Dysfunctional education

- Unfriendly business environment

- High unemployment rate

The extensive National Economic Empowerment and Development

Strategy (NEEDS) reform programme enacted in 2004 under former President Olusegun Obasanjo and continuing today has partly succeeded in correcting some of the imbalances of the Nigerian economy. Nevertheless, given Nigeria's entrenched economic disparities, an entrepreneurial revolution is the veritable last recourse for a country supposedly committed to rejoining the mainstream of economic growth. Nigeria is a signatory to the UN Millennial Declaration of 2000 that proposes universal basic human rights to health, shelter, education and security by 2015. Nigeria has also announced plans of a more ambitious nature that involve taking the country to the top 20 world economies by 2020. While these goals by themselves are not unattainable, they clearly stretch all available projection models and call for massive political reorientation, perseverance and flexibility of imagination and implementation.

The World Bank's Country Partnership Strategy (CPS) for Nigeria outlines basic requirements for sustainable growth: (i) improving governance; (ii) maintaining non-oil growth; and (iii) promoting human development. (World Bank) The strategy is similar to that contained in Nigeria's NEEDS intended to promote economic recovery, growth and development. The four goals of the (2004-2007) NEEDS strategy are poverty reduction, wealth creation, employment generation, and value re-orientation. The goals are grounded in a policy framework of empowering people and improving social delivery; fostering private sector led growth through creating the appropriate enabling environment; and enhancing the efficiency and effectiveness of government, by changing the way government does its work. (IMF).

The World Bank's CPS and Nigeria's NEEDS strategies serve as a summary of key initiatives that the government must focus on in order to drive a sustainable entrepreneurial revolution. These initiatives include:

- Creating a collective socio-economic atmosphere that encourages entrepreneurial development to its fullest and widest capability. This includes tackling infrastructure deficits (in roads, power and communications) that elevate both the cost of doing business and mortality rates.

- Addressing systemic imbalances in terms of policy design and implementation, together with effective measures against institutional corruption.

- Re-calibrating the education system to concentrate on business administration, vocational and practical skills development training.

- Enhancing tax relief and access to venture capital for small business operations by means of promoting lending through equity instead of debt.

- Increasing co-operation among the government, private sector and aid agencies as a means of creating a mass base of viable enterprises.

- Maintaining political stability and the authority of democratic institutions by building social consensus on important policy issues.

Most of the positive strides that Nigeria has managed to pull off in recent years are because of significant strategy redirection's along the above mentioned lines. While these policy initiatives reflect commitment to major national goals, the eventual degree of success is uncertain. The only certainty, to borrow from the US President's proclamation, is that Nigeria's future rests majorly on its ability to nurture and realise the imagination of its entrepreneurs. Before the current global financial crisis set in, Nigeria had been successful in achieving substantial positive change in its overall balance sheets through a process of re-prioritisation and economic reform since 1999. Policy initiatives, including privatisation of several steel, petrochemical, mining and port entities, helped develop the non-oil sector, bring down inflation and boost international currency reserves. Nigeria also successfully negotiated with the London and Paris clubs to do away with a large part of its foreign debt. However, even during periods of relative prosperity, poverty levels remained unabated in the broadest sense, and actually worsened during successive positive growth periods.

Between 1972 and 1980, for instance, the Nigerian per capita income shot up from $1,300 to $2,900 based on rapidly escalating oil prices. A subsequent decline in global oil revenues dragged down per capita income, consumption and expenditure. However, Nigeria neglected investment in human development projects and continued to pump borrowed finances into capital-intensive enterprises. The fallout was that the dramatic rise in national fortunes bypassed the majority of Nigerians, as evident from the negligible rise in per capita consumption figures for the same period. Despite its plentiful resources and oil wealth, poverty is widespread in Nigeria. The country is now considered one of the 20 poorest countries in the world. Over 70 per cent of the population is classified as poor, with 35 per cent living in absolute poverty. The situation is especially severe in rural areas, due to a limited or non-existent social services and public infrastructure. (Rural Poverty Portal)

The differential effect on poverty levels in rural and urban areas for the coinciding period is equally startling. Because of a simultaneous worsening of income distribution, rural poverty declined slightly while the number of urban poor increased. However, the worst-off were also the worst losers, as the population living in extreme poverty across Nigeria swelled from 10 million to 14 million.(World Bank). The obvious explanation behind this is that policy makers sorely failed to share the increase in wealth equitably.

Until 1985, a variety of local factors (political turmoil, social unrest and mismanagement of state assets) and foreign influences (falling oil prices) were responsible for increasing poverty and a widening disparity between rural and urban incomes. Even by 1995, per capita income and consumption remained lower than at the beginning of the oil boom in the 1970s. It was only towards the end of the 20th century that Nigeria began to press forward a concerted effort at reform and regulation, made possible by relative political stability and the establishment of a democratically elected government.

The advent of more inclusive policies began with the adoption of measures intended to diversify Nigeria's economy by encouraging the growth of MSMEs. Entrepreneurship is the core ideal of all developed nations that have successfully capitalised on their human and natural resources to drive economic progress. Since the Thatcher-Reagan era of the 1980s, most developed and developing nations the world over have wholeheartedly embraced entrepreneurship as the key to economic growth and diversification.

For Nigeria, caught in its paradox of mass poverty amongst great wealth, the entrepreneurial revolution holds tremendous relevance and opportunity. As President Kagame makes clear in the case of Rwanda, an important first step for Nigeria is the need for fundamental changes in outlook and practices with regards to promoting entrepreneurship as a means to permanently overcoming poverty and achieving grassroots development. Too many individuals seek security in the familiar scramble for government jobs; they lack the mindset of entrepreneurial risk taking; they lack self-belief. Too many individuals depend on their families and the government in good and bad times. Instead of striving to change their circumstances, they constantly blame and complain. They have an entitlement mentality. Too many individuals have an unproductive mindset. This attitude cannot drive the entrepreneurial, revolutionary, transformation of Nigeria's economy.

Of equivalent importance is upgrading infrastructure and improving access to social services, especially health and education. Engineering a country-wide entrepreneurial spirit also calls for simultaneous national reorientation, in a way that reflects Nigeria's historical social philosophies and structures of mutual assistance. This reorientation must be the basis for designing and implementing policies to tackle the widespread poverty in urban and rural areas.

Nigeria's future economic success depends on creativity and perseverance. It is necessary to design locally applicable solutions for accelerated economic growth. In view of Nigeria economic realities, these solutions once found will need persistent and flexible implementation. It is certainly not going to be an easy job bringing about and sustaining an entrepreneurial spirit in Nigerian affairs. Nevertheless, unless the country manages to do just that, the chances of Nigeria becoming a global economic powerhouse are slim.

MSMEs vs. Large Enterprises: Key Lessons from History and the Way Forward for Nigeria

Recent economic history in Nigeria and across the globe highlights the fact that large enterprises are obviously not the way to pursue Nigeria's development goals. This is made clear by the recent collapse of numerous large enterprises in diverse economic environments around the world. For a nation of 150 million people - more than half of them living in poverty – the MSMEs sector is one that holds out immense promise of durable development. Of critical importance here is the fact that MSMEs offer a distinct macroeconomic profile and potential, and are not merely scaled-down versions of larger enterprises. The financial flexibility, employment potential and innovative capacity of MSMEs have contributed substantially to both developed and developing economies.

Allowing for local and circumstantial variables, MSMEs have shown greater profitability across national barriers owing to higher human capital efficiency and product transformation capacity.
On the flip side, small enterprises suffer two basic disadvantages that large enterprises by definition are without: elevated rates of employee costs as well as working capital requirements. Large enterprises have lower costs per unit turnover and substantially larger cash flow capacities. Moreover, MSMEs represent a high risk factor in terms of debt repayment capacity, often because of inadequate financial know-how and limited access to guidance and consultation. Long term success of MSMEs is additionally contingent upon a heightened degree of financial flexibility that enables rapid adaptation to changing market needs.

The disappointment with large scale, capital intensive and often import-dependent businesses had been growing long before the current global economic downturn set in. While Nigeria has a lot to blame regarding its experience with large enterprises, reports of their diminishing impact on inclusive economic growth is emerging unmistakably from across the globe. As new economic realities begin to hold sway, slowly but surely the practicality of mammoth ventures running on gigantic employee and capital turnovers is slipping away.
MSMEs, on the contrary, hold out a multitude of short and long term benefits that are of especial relevance to Nigeria. These benefits include wider utilisation of natural and human resources, rural development, increased savings and greater regional balance. A policy shift in favour of the rapid promotion of smaller enterprises is a priority for Nigeria. There are, certainly, significant challenges in this direction, none more pressing than the need to create a mindset

change among Nigerians with regards to grassroots entrepreneurship. Further practical problems are in the form of skilled manpower shortage, a high enterprise mortality rate and major infra-structural deficiencies. Improving availability and access to finance and equity remains the most critical challenge to efforts to stimulate healthy MSME sector growth.

Challenges Facing MSMEs in Nigeria

During Nigeria's severe economic decline in the 1980s and 1990s, the environment grew increasingly unfavourable for entrepreneurial success. Indeed, the business environment in the whole of Africa is crippled with massive infrastructure shortfalls that result in the continent's high enterprise mortality rate. Significantly, the rate of failure affects older and new entrants alike. A leading cause is almost always infrastructure deficits that critically hamper genuine economic growth and productivity. Nigeria likewise suffers from endemic infra-structural woes with regards to roads, communication and especially power (small and large businesses alike across the country rely heavily, and at times exclusively, on backup electricity).

There have been no worthwhile attempts so far to radically upgrade the power sector, or attract private investment. Part of the reason these and other objectives have since been frustrated is the huge difference between policy and execution, a problem of developing nations in general. In Nigeria, it is a key concern because of its close relation to another national catastrophe: widespread bureaucratic corruption. Corruption permeates every government institution and parastatals in Nigeria. International aid agencies claim much of the failure of Nigeria's economic and poverty alleviation initiatives is due to an intractable bureaucracy that has steadily resisted efficient and fair practices. At the administrative level, Nigeria needs radical changes in fiscal, monetary and industrial policies to both promote new enterprises and aid existing ones. A core problem is the limited to capital markets for MSMEs.

Nigerian's, like entrepreneurs across the globe, understand that entrepreneurship is not something you simply wake up and do. It takes the right environment and, most importantly, the right financial assistance, both of which are major obstacles to entrepreneurial pursuits in Nigeria. 73% of Nigerian's polled said that it is not easy to obtain a loan in Nigeria and thus this will be one of the deciding factors that will stop them from fulfilling their entrepreneurial dreams. Furthermore, 59% of Nigerian's claim that the government, although trying to promote entrepreneurialism, does not make it easy enough to start a business. The filing process is simply too complex as well as the fluctuating tax laws.

Nigerian's, like all entrepreneurs, are worried that economic policies will change in the future and come back to bite derail their investments of money and time in their businesses. (Gallup) At different times, the government has deregulated oil prices, disinvested public sector undertakings, created special economic zones and passed assorted legislation to encourage enterprise development. While some of these measures are starting to show positive results, many have been largely ineffective and others have completely collapsed.

Optimism is one of the most important ingredients to any successful enterprise and, as reported by Gallup Inc, Nigerians are certainly not lacking in hope. In fact, 67% of Nigerians have thought about starting their own business, the highest rate in West Africa. Out of those 67%, 45% have plans to start a business in the next year and 80% believe that their businesses will do well in their country. Furthermore, 75% believe they will be able to find qualified workers and 56% believe that the Government will allow them to make a lot of money. All of this optimism is most certainly a clear indication of how entrepreneurial development will expand in Nigeria's near future. (Gallup)

A recent collection of essays on entrepreneurial innovation in developing economies, titled *'Lessons from the Poor'*, mentions an aspect of Nigerian clothing design. Examining the traditional *adire* dye industry, author Thompson Ayodele reports that the bottom 19% of entrepreneurs polled for the study earned more than state and federal civil servants. This finding is instructive. It provides a classic instance of entrepreneurial spirit, describing the transformation of an established Yoruba craft into a venture for wealth creation and employment generation. It also reflects the serious imbalances that plague Nigeria's economy.

The Nigerian government must effect swift fiscal, monetary and industrial policy changes in order to capitalise on its huge MSME potential. A lot depends on the effective management of its human resource capital – its sizeable population that has been traditionally dependent on extremely small, subsistence-level enterprises. The fate of Nigeria's ambitious economic goals, and efforts to promote political stability and social cohesion through policies to alleviate mass urban and rural poverty, rest largely on the country's ability to utilise this human talent to drive tangible economic growth. This is clearly highlighted as regards the situation of Nigeria's youth and female populations.

Entrepreneurialism: The Solution for Combating Youth Militancy and Crime in Nigeria

Nigeria's population is overwhelmingly young; half the population is under 20 years old. As is broadly recognised, there are important social, political and public policy consequences of a country's age structure. For example, countries with young populations (high percentage under age 15) need to invest more in education, while countries with older populations (high percentage ages 65 and over) need to invest more in healthcare. Also a large young adult population unable to find employment can lead to political unrest.

This has proven to be the case in Nigeria, both in the Niger Delta and in other communities across the country.

Population Profiles of Nigeria and Selected Countries – 2010

Country	Population/World Rank		Age Structure	Median age - years	Growth rate/World Rank	
Nigeria	152,217,341	8	**0-14 years** 41.2% **15-64 years** 55.7% **65 years and over**: 3.1%	19.1	1.966%	60
Egypt	80,471,869	16	**0-14 years** 32.8% **15-64 years** 62.8 **65 years and over**: 4.4%	24.0	1.997%	58
South Africa	49,109,107	25	**0-14 years** 28.6 **15-64 years** 65.9 **65 years and over**: 5.5%	24.7	-0.051%	203
Brazil	201,103,330	5	**0-14 years** 26.5% **15-64 years** 66.9% **65 years and over**: 6.6%	28.9	1.166%	109
China	1,330,141,29 5	1	**0-14 years** 17.9% **15-64 years** 73.4% **65 years and over**: 8.6%	35.2	0.494%	153
India	1,173,108,01 8	2	**0-14 years** 30.1% **15-64 years** 64.6% **65 years and over**: 5.3%	25.9	1.376%	90
USA	310,232,863	3	**0-14 years** 20.1% **15-64 years** 66.9% **65 years and over**: 13%	36.8	0.970%	123

Source: Compiled by author from data in Central Intelligence Agency, The World Fact Book, pages for Nigeria, Egypt, South Africa, Brazil, China, United States, https://www.cia.gov/library/publications/the-world-factbook/geos/ni.html, accessed August 5, 2010

The volatile Niger Delta region - a network of shallow creeks leading to the Gulf of Guinea - is both the greatest boon and bane for Nigeria's economy, and the undisputed hotbed of militant activity in all of West Africa. The discovery of vast hydrocarbon reserves in the area and the subsequent oil boom of the 1970s resulted in widespread destruction of agriculture, together with extensive displacement of rural communities from fertile lands without adequate compensation. The genesis of conflict and militancy in the Niger Delta goes back to youth restiveness in the early years of the country's independence driven by injustices surrounding the distribution of oil wealth.

A secondary cause was severe environmental pollution from oil explorations that devastated the local ecology and rendered vast swathes of territory along the Gulf of Guinea uncultivable. Together, these causes transformed fledgling community conflicts in the Delta region (rife throughout military rule between 1983 and 1999) into hardcore criminal activities by the turn of the last century. Against expectations, the return of democratic governance only served to further proliferate and deepen the crisis. While Nigeria's "petro-violence" is read by many as a just fight against repressive practices of the federal government and western oil companies, there is little debate over the magnitude of its impact on national fortunes.

As stated earlier, bombings, kidnappings and oil-field raids continue to cause an estimated $1 billion in monthly oil revenue losses. Mounting attacks on the oil infrastructure over the past few years have restricted production to 66% of the installed capacity of 3 million barrels per day. This has impacted oil prices, driving them to record highs in recent years, before the current downturn in the global economy. Understandably, there are considerable global and regional implications surrounding Nigeria's attempts to halt the violence through state intervention and peace initiatives. Growth in sub-Saharan Africa's largest economy is critically dependent on containing unrest in the Niger Delta. Unemployment, however, is only one of many reasons behind youth unrest across the country and in the Delta region in particular. Others include:

- Lack of economic support activities and training programmes.
- Marginal youth participation in community decision making.

- Administrative failure, official negligence and corruption.

- Insufficient humanitarian and social welfare initiatives.

- High cost of living and failure to meet basic needs.

- Lack of education, socio-political empowerment and self esteem.

- Drug abuse and violence; inadequate recreational facilities.

- Problems of good governance in the Niger Delta.

- Over exposure to negative western cultures.

- Over exposure to the culture of greed.

- Ethnicity and lack of National consciousness.

Over the past decade, militants have abducted hundreds of foreign workers employed in the Niger Delta, forcing oil, telecom and construction companies to declare *force majeure* on multiple ongoing contracts and withdraw non-essential staff from vital installations. The security situation growing out of area is now a major deterrent to new investment, and not just in the oil sector or in the Delta. The larger repercussion of the Niger Delta crisis has been on Nigeria's efforts to achieve rapid and sustainable development through an entrepreneurial revolution.

Clearly, that effort faces its biggest challenge from the petro-violence. Initiatives to address the violence and develop the Niger Delta region, like the Niger Delta Development Commission (NDDC), have had only limited success in the areas of youth development and conflict resolution, largely due to bureaucratic inefficiency, inconsistent policies and the absence of regulatory frameworks. Because of its complex geopolitical and economic history, youth empowerment in Nigeria demands a holistic approach focused on certain key issues:

- Overhaul of the education system with specific emphasis on skills development and vocational training.

- Provision of meaningful employment and occupational avenues that are consistent with local realities.

- Administrative reforms that focus on transparency and accountability in youth policy implementation.

- Rehabilitation programmes that successfully wean away militants from violence and into economically productive endeavours.

- Instilling attitudes of national pride among the youth through creatively designed outreach programmes.

- Promoting extensive youth entrepreneurship by means of financial concessions, technical assistance and grants-in-aid.

- Safety-net social policies that persuade the coming generation of Nigerian youth away from crime and violence.

- Effective poverty alleviation programmes that focus on enterprise development as a viable means to legitimate prosperity.

- Mobilisation of the youth workforce to promote rapid entrepreneurial development in rural and urban areas alike.

- Improvement in per capita income, standard of living and related human development indices through implementation of informed social and economic policy changes.

To develop a nation of entrepreneurs, there must be a multi-sectoral, multi-level and multi-phase undertaking that begins with a collective resolve to get out of the old mould of doing things. There must be a radical and co-ordinated attempt to accelerate wealth creation through the promotion of innovative business practices. Nigeria's long-term goals are unachievable without the whole-hearted participation of its sizeable youth population.

There is a critical shortage of legitimate jobs in Nigeria, which has resulted in a rise in poverty which in turn readily lends itself to unrest and violence due to a high youth population. As the youth are consumed with how to find their daily bread, they tend to engage in criminal activities – political thuggery, oil bunkering, armed robbery, thieving, war mongering, banditry, etc. Technology is the fastest growing sector in Nigeria and has presented "419" scam artists with the dubious opportunity of scamming people thousands of miles away out of their hard earned income, gaining international notoriety for Nigeria. Further, there are organised crime operations that not only include internet scams, but also drug trafficking and racketeering, that have been growing in number since the 1980s.

If youth are trained and supported in business start-up and growth, they can create legitimate self-employment opportunities, rather than resorting to crime. By providing opportunity, young individuals can look ahead to a viable economic future rather than one mired in poverty. Although there are those individuals that will turn to crime no matter what legitimate opportunities may exist, overall entrepreneurial development will lead to a reduction in crime.

This is a common sense observation, because many within Nigeria are resorting to theft and other crimes in order to survive not because they are sociopaths.

> When women are fully involved, the benefits can be seen
> immediately: families are healthier and better fed; their
> income, savings and reinvestment go up. And what is true of
> families is also true of communities and, in the long run, of
> whole countries (Kofi Annan)

International observers and aid agencies frequently cite the case of Africa's most populous nation when it comes to highlighting women's issues. Nigeria's future growth prospects are irrevocably tied to the status of its women and its ability to adequately leverage their considerable economic potential.

In this light, the following are some of the key issues the country's government and policy makers need to explore:

- Legal reforms guaranteeing equal rights of women to ownership, property and financial control. Social reforms to enforce humane treatment of women and their worthwhile participation in the development of their families and communities.

- Development of special entrepreneurial initiatives that focus on unbiased participation of women in gainful enterprises and make adequate allowances for their socio-cultural, economic and legal constraints.

- Redrawing budgetary allowances and state expenditure outlays to specifically improve gender equality and promote increased participation of women in new and existing entrepreneurial activities.

- Enhanced collaboration between women and financial, policy and aid agencies through innovative models that takes women's lack of formal training and business expertise into account.

- Minimise failure-rates for enterprises involving women through ongoing technical and financial assistance, with in-built frameworks for efficiency monitoring and continuous survey.

- Improved communication and co-operation between women entrepreneurs across related sectors to assist creation of resource pools and sharing of expertise and technical support.

- Improved accountability on women's issues at both state and federal levels through evaluation of official programmes.

These points are by no means exhaustive in terms of the issues facing Nigerian women, but they do outline in broad strokes the efforts necessary to successfully empower and include them in the process of sustainable growth. Despite their past and present condition, Nigerian women hold one of the keys to the country's long-term prosperity.

Nigerian women have just as much innate chance as Nigerian men to succeed in the world of business. However, there are barriers between women and success, chief among which is the mentality that women are inferior to men. Women are impoverished because of socio-cultural and institutional barriers stacked against them. For example, the economic condition of the country has forced most poor parents to prefer the education of boys rather than girls despite a subsidised public education system. And in an economy with high unemployment rates, women suffer more as they are regarded as less credible applicants for government and corporate jobs. Thus entrepreneurship offers one of the few viable options for women for economic empowerment.

Pursuing the Entrepreneurial Revolution in Nigeria

In order for an entrepreneurial revolution to take off, key aspects of the social, economic, and policy framework must be restructured to meet the needs of entrepreneurs. These facets include the privatisation of government owned businesses (parastatals), the education system, the information technology infrastructure, the credit and banking system, and public safety.

Privatisation and the Entrepreneurial Revolution

Across Africa, privatisation has become the guiding principle for countries trying to develop dynamic private sectors and expand their economies. Yet, countries continue to face tough challenges in terms of disappointing social indicators, deficient infrastructure and marginal, underdeveloped economies.

Nigeria has pursued major privatisation initiatives in the effort to grow and diversify its economy. The thrust of the government's endeavours has been on curbing state expenditure and involvement in direct economic production, and the promotion of local and foreign investment. The broad parameters of Nigeria's privatisation initiative drew on past successes elsewhere in the world, from the UK to Russia, and from Europe to the USA and Asia. Nigeria's formal introduction with the concept came about with the Privatisation and Commercialisation Decree of 1988. In 1999, the Bureau of Public Enterprise (BSE) was set up by federal government enactment to prepare and implement the government's privatisation policies. Embarrassingly, a number of the first privatisation deals ended in fiasco.

The administration of President Obasanjo sold off two refineries to a private consortium, but the sale was later overturned by the administration of President Yar'Adua over allegations of wrongdoing. Subsequent efforts to privatise refineries have stalled. Divestment of the Nigerian public sector telecom monopoly NITEL ended in disaster when the company suffered huge losses and failed debt obligations, forcing the government to retake control.

The now defunct national carrier, Nigerian Airways, likewise failed to take off despite several attempts at commercialisation. Besides indicating ineptitude in policy and implementation, these instances, more importantly, serve to highlight the extensive failure of big business in Nigeria.

Rapid enterprise development in an atmosphere conducive to private sector growth is the only way Nigeria can hope to achieve it MDGs commitments or its indigenous Vision 2020 goals. The benefits arising out of privatisation are too crucial for Nigeria to ignore in the context of its long-term growth plans:

- Depending on prudent implementation, privatisation can help strengthen capital markets by widening local ownership through reservation of shares for citizens.
- Many governments have successfully reduced national debt by raising money through disinvestment and related instruments, curbing the need for subsidies and tax concessions.

- Privatisation engenders healthy competition that helps expand markets, establishes best practices and improves production and service standards.

- World Bank research confirms substantial performance improvement in private enterprises with the removal of administrative constraints typical of public sector operation.

- Developing countries like India and Brazil with strong commitment to free markets have succeeded in acquiring massive foreign investment by privatising public sector monopolies.

Considering its past experiences, it is imperative that Nigeria formulate effective public sector reforms before pushing ahead with any further sale of public assets. Moreover, such measure must be undertaken as part of a larger effort at promoting economic efficiency.

Education for the Entrepreneurial Revolution

In a July 2008 interview, a newspaper reporter asked Ifeanyi Okoye, a senior officer of the Manufacturers' Association of Nigeria: "[are] our young graduates… not employable anymore?" He responded, "You cannot talk to a graduate and be convinced that he is one." (Edike) This response is a strong indictment of the state of Nigerian education. It spotlights problems plaguing the Nigerian educational system which include: lack of cohesive policies on educational standards, inadequate infrastructure, the lack of qualified instructors, overpopulation of substandard educational institutions, and a lack of regulation of the education industry. The problems of education contribute to the major challenges of the technical and professional brain-drain and shortages of highly skilled manpower that continue to cripple domestic efforts to achieve rapid, sustainable growth. For qualified youths looking for jobs, it explains the prolonged and intensive pre-recruitment tests that Nigerian corporate houses insist on before hiring local talent.

Western education first came to Nigeria with missionaries in the middle of the 19th Century, who set up the country's first schools. By the time Nigerians declared independence from colonial rule in 1960, there were three distinct education systems in operation: indigenous community training and apprenticeship in rural areas, schools of Islamic learning, and formal western-inspired education. Arguably, formal western education thrived in the decades of the 1960s and 1970s until the collapse of global oil prices in the early 1980s forced huge reductions in government spending on education. The outcome was a gradual degradation at all levels of learning, from primary schools to universities, and a corresponding fall in literacy rates. According to a 2004 report, the overall literacy rate had fallen from almost 72% in 1991 to 64% at the end of the last century. (UNDP) Improving the level and type of education is essential for the growth and diversification of Nigeria's economy. There is also well-established relationship between increasing literacy and decreasing the level of individual and household poverty.

The following are some of the biggest challenges facing Nigerian education:

- Inadequate infrastructure, manpower, and equipment across all levels of education, from primary to tertiary.

- Under-funding from government, which continues to shrivel resources and stunt growth in the sector.

- Chronic late payment of teachers.

- Student inappropriate behaviour; teacher ethical violations.

- Restrained private participation and almost exclusive dependence on government aid.

- Issues of responsibility and control due to overlapping federal, state, and local government jurisdiction.

- Insufficient use of information and communication technologies, modern equipment and innovative methods of teaching.

- Absence of curricula relevant to national manpower requirements and human development goals.

In the pursuit of an entrepreneurial revolution in Nigeria, several interrelated educational initiatives need to be pursues expeditiously:

- The government must design broad strategies to revive and develop the education system in tune with socio-economic realities and the country's long-term growth targets.

- Educational curricula should instruct Nigerians to become the best entrepreneurs in the world. Micro businesses benefit from science and technology.

- Investment in education has to be substantially enhanced; expenditure models need to be reworked to allow for universal basic education together with effective vocational training.

- A substantial portion of the investment must go for infrastructure development and training and orientation programmes for teachers at all levels.

- Radical transformation of higher education must be achieved with the aim of providing socially relevant skills to unemployed youths in both rural and urban areas.

- Development of sound tertiary institutions to provide quality skills education and training to internationally acceptable standards is vital.

- Government must create conditions for increased participation by the private sector and civil-society organisations in educational reform and execution.

- Effective monitoring and supervision of budgetary allowances in education must be made a priority to ensure accountable utilisation of resources.

Infrastructure Development and the Entrepreneurial Revolution

The general state of infrastructure across the African continent and especially sub-Saharan Africa is acutely underdeveloped. With the exception of South Africa, the entire region is bogged down by severe infrastructure deficiencies that have frustrated development programmes and marred growth prospects. Ifeanyi Okoye, the senior officer of the Manufacturers' Association of Nigeria decries the deficient infrastructure, as well as the high cost of credit: the lack of a supporting environment for entrepreneurs makes manufacturing in Nigeria akin to "sending citizens to war without arms." (Edike)

In June 2009 the World Bank approved a $1 billion loan for Nigeria to fund multiple development programmes including expansion and enhancement of the country's massively deficient power sector. An amount of $200 million was earmarked for investment in networking and technical upgrades to improve electric supply. While this concessionary, interest-free funding is welcome, it amounts to a tiny fraction of Nigeria's overall investment requirement in infrastructure. In August 2008, the Nigerian Debt Management Office (DMO) revealed that the country needed at least $100 billion in investment to develop four key infrastructure areas - power, rail, roads and oil & gas. The figure was calculated to align with the ambitious national goal of taking Nigeria to the top-20 world economies by 2020. Of the four sectors mentioned, power alone would require an estimated investment of between $18 and $20 billion over the next ten years. Currently only 40% of Nigerians have access to electricity.

The collapse of basic infrastructure and social services was set off in the 1980s, when the static oil economy wiped out traditional and emerging livelihoods, creating rampant unemployment, poverty and degraded living standards. Infrastructure declined; for instance, the rail network is in shambles and today accounts for only 1% of national transportation. The port service likewise suffers severe bottlenecks and inadequate capacity. The over 100,000 km long road network is in disrepair at best and barely usable at worst. Because of Nigeria's strategic location and the abundance of its natural resources, infrastructure development in the country has pan-African relevance. The whole of the West African receives very nominal foreign private investment in infrastructure due to reasons ranging from high foreign exchange risks to low creditworthiness. For the most part, the region is dependent on grants-in-aid and soft loans from international development agencies to finance infrastructure investments. Increasing foreign investment on infrastructure, while simultaneously developing avenues for credible local finance is a daunting task. Nigeria needs to lead the way in enhancing access to equity debt as a means of attracting projects with viable private participation.

For Nigeria, the larger impact of infrastructure deficits is the high cost of doing business, for large corporations and small enterprises alike. The government of former President Yar'Adua listed infrastructure development as a cornerstone component of the 7 Point Agenda for realisation of the 2020 goals as well as the Millennium Development targets.

Venture Capitalism and the Entrepreneurial Revolution

The government's focus on MSME development prompted a unique voluntary initiative at the turn of the last century when the Nigerian Bankers' Committee launched the Small and Medium Enterprise Equity (SMEEIS) scheme. Billed as an attempt to promote entrepreneurial expansion, the scheme required all locally operating commercial banks to earmark 10% of pre-tax profits for equity investment in small and medium enterprises. Over N18 billion had been set aside by 2003, but less than 25% the funds were utilised, due to the lack of viable projects and general reluctance toward equity partnership. Its large population and market size confers tremendous potential on the Nigerian economy. Past experience argues against relying on big businesses, which have had a dismal track record and a high-failure rate under both private and public operation. Undeniably, the fate of Nigeria's long term goals rests on rapid proliferation of MSMEs and their ability to drive an enterprise revolution that will sufficiently diversify the economy away from oil and reverse decades of stagnation.

The objective is to use MSMEs to deliver sustainable development, employment creation and most importantly, poverty alleviation. This is where venture capitalism derives its significance in the context of Nigeria's long-term ambitions. Private equity investment has been responsible for some of the most notable economic success stories across the globe. Entrepreneurs starting out with angel loans turned India into the largest software exporter in the world.
In South Korea, booming small high-tech businesses bypassed larger firms to lead the country's recovery from the Asian economic crisis. Equity funded enterprises have likewise recorded high growth figures in developing countries from Asia, across Europe and in South America. The global experience with venture capitalism throws up a number of important considerations in terms of providing the right environment for rapid growth.

The following are some of the most important challenges and considerations facing Nigerian policy makers in this regard:

- Establishing a venture capital technical assistance programme to enhance SME performance in diverse economic sectors.

- Institutionalising tax benefits for equity investment to attract foreign investors.

- Focusing equity investment on SMEs that optimise resource utilisation and assist local raw material development.

- Promoting innovative business ideas, processes and techniques that boost both productivity and profitability.

- Hastening industrialisation through equity infusion in high-growth areas like telecommunications and tourism.

Information Technology and the Entrepreneurial Revolution

A 2001-02 analysis of global IT infrastructure ranked Nigeria 75th of 75 surveyed countries. (Centre for International Development) The whole of West Africa suffers from endemic 'information poverty', and Nigeria is no exception. Nigeria obtained its first digital computer in 1963. Installations remained low even after many individual universities, government departments and public sector undertakings had acquired some amount of computing power towards the end of the 1970s. While the number of internet service providers (ISPs) and cyber cafés increased, IT development received meagre official stimulus in the last century. In fact Nigeria had no IT policy until 2001, when it instituted the National IT Development Agency with a $28 million grant. Tasked with making Nigeria "a key player in the Information society", the agency has been widely criticised for ineffectiveness and failure to align with other national policies. Nigeria's IT potential has been significantly underachieved, and consequently, its efforts to drive rapid enterprise development across sectors have fallen short of expectations.

There are over 500,000 businesses operating across the country, engaged in manufacturing, services, retail and wholesale. Most of these companies stand to benefit from IT products, services, or training. Nigerian software developers, in turn, stand to both contribute to and gain immensely from this situation. The growth curve for indigenously-developed IT is potentially steep. Potential also exists for the small business sector to shake things up for the entire economy through intelligent harnessing of IT tools. For instance, a 2005 AC Nielsen survey found that the online auction and sales site eBay had a "significant impact" on the growth of small business in the USA.

In the first six months of that year, eBay entrepreneurs in the US sold more than $10 billion worth of merchandise. (Ebay) The report goes on to say that over 400,000 American users relied on sales through the web-site as a primary or secondary source of income. These findings represent an achievable model of small business development for Nigeria, but one that depends vitally on wider access to IT and acquaintance with internet usage. Nigerian entrepreneurs in diverse economic sectors can develop thriving businesses, generating employment and boosting local economies, by accessing international markets online.

Even better inspiration comes from India, where the software industry has outperformed global competition hands down. The industry grew exponentially from $150 million in 1991 to $5.7 billion in 2000, while projected revenue for 2008 stood at a mammoth $87 billion, or 7.5% of GDP.   A government of India report estimated that in 2008:

- Software & Services will contribute over 7.5 % of the overall GDP growth of India.

- IT Exports will account for 35% of the total exports from India.

- Potential for 2.2 million jobs in IT by 2008

- IT industry will attract Foreign Direct Investment (FDI) of U.S. $ 4-5 billion

- Market capitalisation of IT shares will be around U.S. $ 225 billion (Embassy of India)

Actual IT contributions to India's economy were impacted negatively by the global economic crisis which took hold in the second half of 2008. Nevertheless, the point is clear that IT growth and innovation can spur successful entrepreneurial development and economic expansion. Nigeria can take a cue from this internationally acclaimed success story by vigourously tapping into the IT and knowledge industries. Nigeria needs to capitalise on its human resource pool to turn out technically proficient workers who can take the economy to higher rates of growth. If anything, the Indian example is strong proof that IT alone can turn around a country's fortunes.

The following are some of the notably encouraging developments for Nigerian IT so far:

- Nigeria signed the Regional African Satellite Communications Organisation for multimedia telecommunications services in 2001, visibly increasing government participation in IT.

- Multinational corporations have led the way in introducing online banking operations that have begun to catch on with resident and expatriate Nigerians.

- E-commerce initiatives in the B2B and B2C segments have been running successfully, even if most of the IT content and equipment has had to be entirely imported.

- Cyber cafes are common in urban communities.

By themselves, these measures are not enough to promote IT as a growth fundamental. For Nigeria to tap its enterprise potential in time for the 2020 goals requires a massive reinvigoration and rationalisation of its IT development initiatives. The government must realise the importance of developing entrepreneurial capability in the IT sector to ensure inclusive and sustainable growth. Provided it is suitably adjusted to local realities, a digital revolution facilitates poverty eradication by enabling extensive business development and wealth creation. The challenge before Nigeria today is to develop the use of IT and communication technologies in a manner that accords the widest benefits from, and contributions to, national economic growth and diversification.

Nigeria has to undertake several co-ordinated initiatives in order to meet its IT obligations, and more importantly, to drive and capitalise on the digital revolution. The most pressing initiatives are:

- Improving the telecommunications infrastructure, upgrading communication techniques and improving the reach of mobile and fixed-line telephony services across rural and urban areas.

- Enhancing basic computer skills and advanced IT education through a structured overhaul of the education system; specific focus on tertiary institutions offering engineering programmes.

- Patronising indigenous software over imports, funding research and promoting private and public sector co-operation for innovation and enterprise in the IT sector.

- Developing sound policies that propagate IT as a crucial component of business culture; fostering IT-enabled practices as a means of governance and administrative optimisation.

- Active promotion of procedures that introduce computerisation and IT to the industrial process, through use of advanced digital technologies and office automation systems.

Security and the Rule of Law in the Entrepreneurial Revolution

Nigeria's history of conflict and bloodshed began not long after its independence from British colonial rule in 1960. Six years later, Army officers executed the then Prime Minister and two of his cabinet colleagues in the country's first of many coup d'etats. Political upheaval stoked social fires as religious, ethnic and regional disparities overflowed to create a climate of official persecution and brutal governance. The string of military take overs continued into the 1990s, until the very end of the last century, when the first peaceful transition to civilian power brought back some degree of political normalcy to the nation.

As significant a development as it was, the return of relative political stability did not bring about the automatic cessation of internal divides and hostilities that one might have wished. Nigeria's volatile economic and political unity continues to be a threat to its security and stability. The existence of potentially destabilising forces within its boundaries has long been obvious to the international community. Radical separatist groups, some demanding devolution and others autonomy, have sprung up across both northern and southern territories. Further, growing Islamic extremism is another point of grave concern. The cumulative socio-economic impact of these activities has been tremendous. To some scholars, the Nigerian paradox accounts for the insidious criminal activity in the country – the fact that over half of the 150 million Nigerians are poor, while an estimated 35% of the population lives in extreme poverty in an oil-producing country. The spectrum of criminal activity in Nigeria is extensive and diverse. The country's strategic location makes it a key transit point for a host of illegal networks, including major international drug routes. Administrative inefficiency and malpractice's fed by the billions in annual petrodollar profits have also made it a centre of massive economic corruption and fraud.

In fact, the country was listed by the inter-governmental Financial Action Task Force as a noncooperative country until 2006, when it finally issued formal commitments to fight economic crime. Nigerian scams called 419s are known for ingenious ways of targeting foreigners across the globe and causing both monetary loss as well as personal harm. The condition is much more unsettling at the street level, where armed assault, burglary, kidnappings and extortion, involving both individuals and gangs, are everyday occurrences across the country.

The US state department reports 44 abductions of foreign oil workers from Nigeria since 2008. Reasons behind the lawless disrepair in Nigeria's state of affairs include:

- Economic disparities that grew out of non-inclusive policies and the exclusive dependence on oil, which destroyed indigenous economies and livelihoods, spawned critical levels of inflation and unemployment, and left millions reeling in poverty.

- Political misrule, corruption and neglect of social development projects that over the years alienated the vast majority of Nigerian's, amplified urban-rural divides and deepened fractures along religious and ethnic lines.

- Flaws in the judicial and law enforcement process, largely due to the existence of multiple criminal justice systems based on often contradicting but separately applicable penal codes, Islamic edicts and customary laws.

- Legislative emasculation brought on by decades of military rule. This severely curtails the government's ability to enforce relevant policies and gain sufficient supervision and oversight of core development programmes.

The Nigerian federal government suffered an estimated $20 billion shortfall in oil production and export revenues in 2008 due to militant violence in the Niger Delta region. While this is a considerable amount, it pales in comparison with the billions more it loses annually to aborted contracts, production delays and business closures because of security issues. Even more significant are the repercussions on latent economic sectors like tourism.

The government admits the possibility of earning more revenue from tourism than it does from oil, and has been involved of late in developing a tourism profile to attract international travellers. Between 2000 and 2004, international air arrivals jumped from 12,000 to 190,000, while the hotel and restaurant sector's contribution to GDP grew from N4.9 billion to N6 billion. Going by such indicators, the Nigerian Tourism Development Corporation is understandably confident of developing the country as a world-class circuit of important monuments, landmarks, nature retreats and heritage sites. Yet, tourism, as a profitable economic activity, is virtually non-existent in this corner of sub-Saharan Africa; hardly surprising considering the long list of nations that have stern advisories against travelling to Nigeria unless absolutely essential.

A similar dictum seems to guide investments flowing into the country. Foreign direct investment (FDI) in Nigeria was over $11 billion in 2009, well under desirable levels considering that most of the funds were concentrated on the oil industry. The security situation is largely to blame for a very small fraction of FDI reaching other sectors, as it is discouraging expatriate Nigerian's from investing in their country of origin. The spectre of violence and lawlessness has proved a strong deterrent against the establishment of business ventures by the Nigerian diaspora, a critical failing that keeps away billions of dollars in potential investment. Where countries like India and China have reaped huge benefits from expatriate investment, Nigeria has been far less fortunate because the risks involved in doing business in the country are too high.

The following are some of the broad and specific measures the government needs to be looking at in order to address the security situation:

- Correcting the deficit in administrative legitimacy by addressing core issues that feed violence and organised crime. Genuine grievances and concerns must be effectively addressed to soothe popular discontent.

- Using economic growth and prosperity at ground levels as a weapon to isolate extremist and criminal elements, effectively denying them the public support and collaboration their operations rely on.

- Enhancing effectiveness of security operations in sensitive areas through better strategy, increased vigilance along industrial clusters and improved co-operation between state and federal law enforcement agencies.

- Re-evaluation of centralised policing in favour of devolved powers for control and deployment of police forces. Nigeria's federal structure and complex state laws make a strong argument in favour of a decentralised police force.

- Maintaining the authority of democratic institutions and the rule of law by increasing transparency in governance; initiating effective measures against corruption and bureaucratic red tape.

The Entrepreneurial Revolution: the Banking and the Financial Sector

In 2009, the Nigerian government was forced to pump $2.6 billion into five troubled banks after discovering their base capitals had plummeted to levels that threatened the entire financial system. The move has awakened deep concerns about the state of affairs in Africa's second largest economy where banking is strategic to financial stability. While it may still be too early to speculate on how this affects investor attitudes, the government is confident in its intervention based on the sheer potential of the economy.

The following are some of major obstacles facing the Nigerian banking industry:

- Unprofitable operations due to liquidity constraints and poor asset qualities.

- Disregard for small and medium savings in favour of large public sector deposits.

- Inept corporate governance, proliferation of unethical practices and non-compliance with regulatory mechanisms.

- Meagre capital base, even for banks that qualify the revised minimum requirement of $15 million for new banks.

- Insolvency, often forced by operating losses that wipe out shareholder investments.

A bank consolidation programme was implemented in 2004 to enhance credit availability to the private sector, especially small businesses. The degree of success attending these policies is perhaps reflected only in comparisons. As of 2004, there were 89 banks operational in Nigeria, the large majority with a capital base of less than $10 million. South Africa, on the other end, had one bank with more branches and assets than all 89 put together.

Nigeria's quest for economic resurgence is inherently tied to the health of its banks. The following are some of the key measures necessary for this sector to help bring about a much-needed entrepreneurial revolution:

- Significant enhancement in the minimum capitalisation for banks, together with phased withdrawal of public sector funds from commercial bank deposits.

- Establishment of a competent regulatory and oversight authority to prevent insider trading and ethical malpractice's and optimise banking efficiency.

- Strengthening of applicable legal frameworks and better enforcement of existing banking laws to avoid fiscal mismanagement and failures.

- Enhanced co-operation between banks and the Economic and Financial Crimes Commission of Nigeria to prevent misconducts and promote transparency.

- Consolidation of banks through mergers and acquisitions to increase availability of finance for long-term infrastructure development projects.

The Entrepreneurial Revolution Must Succeed: Failure is not an Option

Resolving the Nigerian paradox of mass poverty in the midst of bountiful resources centres on realising the economic transformations inherent in a successful entrepreneurial revolution. Economic diversification, exploiting the full potential of natural and human resources, creating jobs to drive down employment, increasing disposable income, and, ultimately alleviating mass poverty are all tied to this revolution. As with the U.S., Brazil, China and India, recovery and growth in Nigeria can be - and can only be – achieved through the massive growth in the number of entrepreneurs. Entrepreneurship is the surest way to recovery and growth. If not an entrepreneurial revolution, the future portends continuing social alienation, economic misery and political instability.

Alternative Route: Social Entrepreneurship

Before ending this overview of the challenges and opportunities for the entrepreneurial revolution in Nigeria, it is worth taking a look at the issue of social entrepreneurship. Social entrepreneurship combines the concept of entrepreneurship with that of doing social good. Social entrepreneurs recognise a social problem and use their business smarts to do something about it. Instead of using their business ventures to make money, they use their businesses to impact society and effect positive change. They do not weigh their success by the size of their bank account but rather on the effect they have on a society. Social entrepreneurs possess the same confidence, intuition and motivation as business entrepreneurs, but they also possess a more generous level of care. Simply put, it is not about the money; it is about changing a system, spreading a solution and helping a society overcome development obstacles.

Many social entrepreneurs tackle problems that governments have failed to adequately address. Social entrepreneurship is all about pursuing a vision for a brighter social tomorrow and just like all entrepreneurship, it involves taking a risk. At risk is not only financial security but also passions and dreams regarding society. In fact, social entrepreneurship is just as important for a growing society as business entrepreneurship is for the economy. Both are needed to grow and diversify the economy, keep the peace and move forward to an improved system.

Examples of Social Entrepreneurship in Nigeria

Social entrepreneurship is quite popular in Nigeria, a country where civil strife, religious turmoil, corruption, greed and deficient economic and educational infrastructure threaten society on a daily basis. Below are three social entrepreneurs focusing their efforts to help Nigerian society and positively endorse a change.

Durojaiye Isaac: Isaac was the recipient of the award Social Entrepreneur of the Year 2005 for the utility of his mobile toilets. Isaac founded the DMT Mobile Toilets in 1999, an organisation that strives to positively impact the economical and environmental health of Nigeria. DMT Mobile Toilets is a commercial enterprise that produces, rents out and maintains safe and sanitary portable toilets. Not only does Isaac's organisation promote sanitation in public health but it also stimulates the economy by providing job opportunities for youth and women. Before Isaac's foundation was established, there were only around 500 public toilets in Nigeria. Under Isaac's social entrepreneurism, public toilets have been installed in high traffic areas and the unemployment rate has been lowered.

Joachim Ezeji: Ezeji is the founder of Rural Africa Water Development Project (RAWDP) that aims to improve the access to clean drinking water in remote Nigerian communities. Ezeji's RAWDP was founded in 2000 and continues to help improve the water system that has been tarnished by oil and other pollutants. Ezeji plays an active role in the social entrepreneurship, acting as the Chief Officer as well as training team members, implementing projects and developing community water infrastructures. Through the RAWDP, Ezeji has helped millions of Nigerians have access to clean, drinkable water.

Ada Onyejike: Onyejike is the founder of Girl Child Art Foundation (GCAF) in Nigeria which uses art to help young women recognise their importance in society. Young women are often devalued, and thus many girls will drop out of school at a young age. Onyejike's foundation aims to promote education and social change through the empowering arts including performing arts, visual arts and creative writing. Onyejike's ambitious project hopes to build confidence in young women, promote the need for education and prevent the spread of HIV in Nigeria. Onyejike's foundation also hopes to shed some light on the daily lives of all women in Nigeria and the societal customs that are devaluing their life including child marriage, trafficking and rape, polygamy and female genital mutilation. What began in 2000 as a small volunteer operation now has programs in over 200 communities. She reaches thousands of women ages 8 to 25 through art, music and dance in an attempt to change her country for the better.

This is what social entrepreneurship is all about. The real prosperity of a nation depends to a large extent on the prosperity of its entrepreneurs. The next chapter looks at the potential for an entrepreneurial revolution in different sectors of the Nigerian economy. What is applicable to Nigeria can be used to benefit other developing countries.

Sources

Adedipe, B., "The Impact of Oil on Nigeria's Economic Policy Formulation" *African Economic Outlook*, 2007

Agba, J. and M. S. Tenuche, "Managing the Global Economic Meltdown in a Consolidated Banking Sector of Nigeria: Rhetorics or Realities," *Current Research Journal of Economic Theory* 2(1): 16-21, 2010.

Ajayi, D. D., "Recent Trends and Patterns in Nigeria's Industrial Development." Council for the Development of Social Science

Research in Africa, *Africa Development*, Vol. XXXII, No. 2, 2007, pp. 139–155.

Akintoye, R. I., & Olowolaju, P. S. "Optimising Macroeconomic Investment Decisions: A Lesson from Nigeria." *European Journal of Scientific Research* Vol.22 No.4, 2008, pp.469-479
Aladekomo, F. O., "Nigeria Educational Policy and Entrepreneurship". *Journal of Social Science*, 9(2): 2004, pp 75-83.

Ayodele, Thompson, "The Nigerian Clothing Design Industry" In *Lessons from the Poor: Triumph of the Entrepreneurial Spirit.* Edited by Alvaro Vargas Llosa. Oakland, CA: The Independent Institute, 2008.
Center for International Development at Harvard University, *The Global Information Technology Report 2001-2002: Readiness for the Networked World,* http://www.cid.harvard.edu/archive/cr/gitrr_030202.html) accessed August 8, 2010

Dowden, Richard. *Africa: Altered States, Ordinary Miracles.* New York: Perseus Books, 2009.

(Ebay), New Study Reveals 724,000 Americans Rely on eBay Sales for Income," http://investor.ebay.com/releasedetail.cfm? releaseid=170073, accessed August 7, 2010
Embassy of India, "India's Information Technology Industry," http://www.indianembassy.org/indiainfo/india_it.htm, accessed August 8, 2010

International Monetary Fund, "Nigeria: Poverty Reduction Strategy Paper—Progress Report," IMF Country Report No. 07/270, August 2007
Kagame, Paul, "The Backbone of a New Rwanda: Entrepreneurship Is the Surest Way" *Innovations,* Winter 2010, Vol. 5, No. 1, Pages 3-6 accessed July 23, 2010

Kayizzi-Mugerwa, Steve. *The African Economy: Policy, Institutions and the Future.* London: Routledge, 1999.
Moshomba, Richard E. *Africa in the Global Economy.* Boulder, CO.: Lynne Rienner , 2000.

Obama, Barack. *State of the Union Address.* 27 January, 2010
OnlineNigeria, "Metallic Minerals,"
http://www.onlinenigeria.com/minerals/?blurb=517, accessed August 9, 2010
UNDP, Millenium Development Goals Report 2004 Nigeria
http://www.undg.org/archive_docs/5430-Nigeria_MDG_Report, accessed August 7, 2010

World Bank, "Nigeria: Poverty in the Midst of Plenty: The Challenge of Growth with Inclusion," Nigeria May 31, 1996

World Bank, *Nigeria: Country Brief - Strategy*
http://web.worldbank.org/Wbsite/External/Countries/Africaext/Niger iaextn

CHAPTER SEVEN

BUILDING THE ENTREPRENEURIAL REVOLUTION AND ERADICATING POVERTY: A SECTORAL ANALYSIS

"The only place where success comes before work is in the dictionary."

Vidal Sassoon

Creating a Culture of Entrepreneurship in Nigeria and throughout Africa

To summarise our core argument in this book: Entrepreneurship is initiated when people are able to produce more than they require and therefore can trade their surpluses. In Nigeria, modern entrepreneurship involving international trade started with the introduction of cash crops such as cocoa and the commercialisation of palm oil during the colonial era. Since independence, Nigeria has depended on oil revenues as the basis of its economy. These revenues barely trickle down to the common man and woman in the village or the street. It was not until recently that the country has diversified from oil dependence and is steering toward a more enterprise based economy. Nigeria is setting its goals very high and has come up with an ambitious plan to turn its economy into one of the 20 biggest in the world in the span of two decades. It has been determined that the main areas of focus are entrepreneurship and information technology sectors.

In order to become a global economic giant, it was recommended that all students in Nigeria should study entrepreneurship as part of their curriculum regardless of their major subject. According to Nigeria's Ministry of Education, the past few years have witnessed 60% of university graduates being unemployed. A large number of these graduates are establishing entrepreneurial ventures; however, research by the Nigerian Investing Commission (NIC) found that a large number of these new business-people are not adept at managing their ventures. This led to the recommendation by NIC to introduce entrepreneurship in all University programs.

There is massive potential for enterprise development in Nigeria. Opportunities exist both in reviving and growing established economic sectors, such as agriculture, and in new sectors offered by the 21st century globalised, technology-driven economy.

This chapter explores economic sector challenges and opportunities for enterprise development across the Nigerian economy.

Agriculture and the Entrepreneurial Revolution

The story of Nigerian agriculture is embedded within the country's political history. Nigeria had a predominantly agricultural economy in the hundred odd years spent under British colonial rule and well into its first decade of independence. In the 1960s, Nigeria was the world's second largest producer of cocoa, the largest exporter of palm oil, and a principal producer and exporter of cotton, rubber and groundnut. Using traditional tools and practices, Nigerian peasants contributed 70% of export revenue and 60% of GDP in the same period. (Lawal) The total food requirement was met almost entirely by local produce and agricultural imports were to the bare minimum.

The oil boom of the 1970s brought drastic change to the country's economic landscape as the discovery of vast oil and gas reserves turned its fortunes overnight. The windfall transformed Nigeria's agricultural landscape into a gigantic oil field criss-crossed by more than 7,000 km of pipelines connecting 6,000 oil wells, two refineries, innumerable flow stations, and export terminals. Nigeria invested tremendously to create a mega oil production network and the investment paid off, with unofficial estimates suggesting Nigeria earned more than $600 billion from oil and gas in the last decade alone.

Unfortunately, the obsession with oil over all other sectors of the economy eventually turned Nigeria's boon into a bane. New found wealth instigated political instability and massive corruption in government circles, and the country suffered successive military coups and civil unrest. Agriculture was one of the first casualties of the oil regime, and by the 1990s, cultivation accounted for just 5% of GDP. (Olagbaju) Farming modernisation and support continued to remain low on the list of national priorities as vast stretches of rural

Nigeria gradually plunged into poverty and food scarcity. Deforestation, soil erosion, and industrial pollution further hastened the downward-spiral of agriculture to the point where it ended up as a subsistence activity.

Rural Nigeria has long been neglected. Public investments in health, education and water supply have been concentrated in the cities. Poor infrastructure impedes the movement of produce, increasing spoilage, the cost of inputs, and, therefore, the cost of production and the prices of marketable produce. Agriculture is the largest contributor to Nigeria's GDP. Nigeria is the world's largest producer of cassava, yam and cow-pea; it is also a major producer of fish. Yet Nigeria imports large amounts of grain, livestock products and fish to feed its population. (Rural Poverty Portal)

The National Poverty Eradication Programme of 2001 identifies agriculture and rural development as its primary area of interest. The fact that all development has to begin from the bottom-up cannot be overemphasised in the context of Nigeria, where a farming boom can ensure not just food supply and exports but also provide industrial raw materials and a market for products.

Agricultural expansion is critical to economic prosperity across Africa, considering the region's crippling poverty levels. For example, a 2003 conference organised by New Partnership for Africa's Development (NEPAD) in South Africa strongly urged the promotion of cassava cultivation as a poverty eradication tool across the continent. The recommendation is based on a strategy that focuses on markets, private sector participation and research to drive a pan-African cassava initiative. What was once a rural staple and famine-reserve food has become a lucrative cash crop. The NEPAD initiative has strong relevance for Nigeria, the world's largest cassava producer. With its large rural population and extensive farmlands, the country boasts unrivalled opportunities of transforming the humble cassava into an industrial raw material for both domestic and international markets. There is a growing and well-justified belief that the crop can transform rural economies, spur rapid economic and industrial growth and assist disadvantaged communities. While production grew steadily between 1980 and 2002 from 10,000 MT to over 35,000 MT, there is room for significant increase by bringing more land under cassava cultivation. Nigeria must take the lead not only in developing better production, harvesting and processing technologies, but also in finding new uses and markets for what is undoubtedly a wonder crop. Nigeria will make a notable stride towards inclusive and sustainable agricultural development simply through the intelligent and judicious promotion of cassava farming.

Nigeria's agricultural potential is enormous partly because over 90% of its 91 million hectares of total land area is arable. While soil fertility is generally estimated on the lower side, the UN Food and Agriculture Organisation (FAO) predicts medium to high yields across the country with optimal utilisation of resources. Combined with Nigeria's substantial rural population traditionally involved in agriculture, this projection translates to gigantic prospects in terms of agricultural productivity and, by extension, economic resurgence.

The following are some of the most urgent requirements for a successful revolution in Nigerian agriculture:

- Active promotion and establishment of agro-based industries that generate employment, sustain local food requirements, and encourage exports.

- Effective steps to modernise and diversify the agricultural economy as a means of buttressing entrepreneurial growth in ancillary sectors.

- Institution of a tariff system that promotes local produce against cheaper imports, together with the removal of institutional barriers against agricultural profitability.

- Subsidies on technologically advanced farm equipment and practices that help boost productivity without any adverse ecological side effects.

- An umbrella poverty alleviation programme designed specifically to promote agrarian reforms while simultaneously improving the quality of life in rural communities.

- Enhanced access to agricultural enterprise loans through a network of regulated lending institutions sympathetic to farming realities.

- Promotion of Adult education programmes designed to help Nigerian farmers upgrade to locally relevant but modern methods of cultivation, marketing and distribution.

- Encouragement of both public and private sector agricultural research aimed at correcting technological constraints faced by local farming communities.

Nigeria's Agro Allied Industry: A Starting Point for the Entrepreneurial Revolution

As part of former president Umaru Yar'Adua's Seven Point Agenda for economic revival and accelerated growth, the Commercial Agriculture Credit Scheme (CACS) was launched. It was designed to provide concessionary funding to small farmers through credit guarantees and interest draw-back support. Initial outlay for the scheme stands at a respectable $1.4 billion, to be disbursed through participating commercial banks. The Nigerian government envisions that the programme would increase farmland output, diversify the revenue base, and provide vital resources and raw material to the manufacturing sector. The idea of agriculture and agro-based industry as a strategy for accelerated economic growth is slowly beginning to take hold.

As stated earlier, the oil boom of the 1970s, caused the marginalisation of agriculture into a labour-intensive, low-productivity subsistence activity that eventually plunged large parts of rural Nigeria into abject poverty. Despite several resuscitation attempts over the decades - including the 1972 National Accelerated Food Programme, the 1976 Operation Feed the Nation, and the Green Revolution initiative of 1980 – the steady descent of agriculture continued until the very end of the last century.
The redirection of agricultural policies affected since the return of democracy in 1999 proved more successful. Under a radical reforms programme, the government targeted rural development with integrated plans for agriculture promotion, rural industrialisation and infrastructure development. This integrated approach has yielded tangible results: Agriculture now leads the country's economic recovery, bouncing back to contribute 42% of GDP by 2009.

Perhaps the most significant thought arising out of this recovery is Nigeria's natural inclination towards farming. Traditional involvement with agriculture and the existence of diverse ecological conditions across the country offers strong potential for growth of a flourishing and suitably inter-linked agro-allied industry. Nigeria's ambitions for accelerated and inclusive economic growth are contingent on achieving a vibrant agriculture sector that can support extensive down-the-line enterprise development and employment. In line with this assessment, the UN Conference on Trade and Development (UNCTAD) expressly recommends the adoption of a national investment policy to diversify the Nigerian economy with a strong focus on agro-allied industries. The fact that this sector is primed to spark off rapid enterprise development in Nigeria is simply undeniable. Enterprise potential exists in almost all areas of local farm production. According to FAO estimates, Nigeria currently produces over 100,000 metric tonnes of kola nut, which finds use in the manufacture of beverages, liquor, and confectionaries. Yet, local processing units are rare and exports are largely limited to fresh and dry nuts with little value addition. Cassava, likewise, has emerged as a major cash crop with untapped potential in industrial use and bio-fuel development. With adequate private sector involvement, commercialised agriculture can not only aid industrialisation and employment generation but also breach the productivity gap and reduce food costs.

The government's intervention in the agro-allied sector must essentially be aimed at creating the right environment for rapid expansion of locally-owned enterprises. However, there are serious challenges in this direction. Industrial processing of agricultural products is almost negligible, existing standards being very basic and often incomparable with export requirements. Post-harvest losses are also very high, assesses at near 50% of total production. (Van Buren) Labour saving production and advanced harvesting and processing technologies are therefore critical for sustained revival of Nigerian agriculture. Moreover, efficient production and marketing systems will prove vital in ensuring high quality standards and competitive prices for both domestic industries and export markets.

In terms of broad parameters, policies for effective development of the agro-allied sector in Nigeria must focus on a number of key considerations:

- Ensuring food security by increasing supply and lowering prices with the specific aim of curbing inflation.

- Enhancing credit access to small farmers and agro-based enterprises at low rates of interest.

- Providing information, support and training for emerging agro-industries and promoting best practices.

- Increasing productivity through promotion of high-growth models in food processing enterprises.

- Prioritising locally available raw materials over imports.

- Removing informal barriers to trade and streamlined manufacturing of agricultural products.

- Promoting greater regulatory co-operation among West African neighbours to increase regional trade.

- Reducing tariffs on goods and services that support the agro-processing sector.

- Enforcing relevant safeguards for agricultural and value-added food products to guard against import surges.

- Building capacity in the private sector and promoting public-private partnership in agro-processing industries.

The Palm Oil Industry and the Entrepreneurial Revolution

Nigeria's once-thriving palm oil industry is often cited as one of the most notable failed economic opportunities in Africa. Use of the oil palm fruit to extract edible oil has been in practice across the continent for centuries, and it remains an essential ingredient in much of West African cuisine. Farmers in the region, who inter-cropped palm oil with other food crops like yam and maize, started the first export trade early in the nineteenth century. Before its end, the industrial revolution in Britain had created a huge demand for palm oil, which by then had found its way to use in candle making and as an industrial lubricant. The economic importance of palm oil grew steadily because of its high yield, leading European colonists to start plantations in Central Africa by 1900. As palm oil found wider use in food-processing and industry, global demand for the commodity surged. By 1982, worldwide palm oil exports had grown to a staggering 2,400,000 million tonnes per annum.

For most of this period, Nigeria held centre stage as one of the largest producers and exporters of palm oil, accounting for more than 40% of global output in the 1950s. At the time of Nigeria's independence in 1960, palm oil contributed 82% of national export revenue. However, the oil boom of the mid-seventies and the subsequent decline of farming proved catastrophic to the sector. By the end of the twentieth century, the Nigerian palm oil harvest had dwindled to just 7% of global production. The once world's largest exporter became a net importer of palm oil, sourcing 180,000 MT of the commodity from international markets to meet local demand.

The bulk of Nigerian palm oil comes from dispersed and semi-wild groves, and through the use of highly outdated manual processing techniques. Several attempts to establish large-scale plantations since the 1960s - including the Cross River State plan and the Oil Palm Belt Rural Development Programme - ended in miserable failure. Currently, 80% of production comes from scattered smallholdings spread over an estimated 1.6 million hectares of land. In contrast, plantations occupy only about 300,000 hectares - most of this coming about over the last decade with private sector investment.

Economic reforms initiated since 1999 succeeded somewhat in nudging the sector out of stagnation. Between 2001 and 2005, palm oil production grew rapidly from 760 MT to 800 MT, while recording a corresponding rise in local consumption due to a 2002 ban on palm oil importation. However, the ban was lifted in 2009, prompting grave misgivings about the fate of the industry and impact on local production. The Plantation Owners Forum has gone so far as to say the move would severely threaten Nigeria's Vision 2020 goals for accelerated economic development. Besides conventional uses in food-processing, every part of the palm tree has economic value that can be employed in a variety of low-cost activities like roofing and wickerwork. Moreover, palm oil is a source of raw material for a whole range of industries; for instance, those involved in the manufacture of detergents, pomades, confectionary fat and margarine. By virtue of this alone it offers massive scope for employment generation and income distribution, to say nothing of other diversified products like palm kernel oil. The industry has therefore been widely regarded as a high-growth business by the private sector. In countries like Malaysia and Indonesia, which together account for 90% of current global exports, palm oil has proved to be a cornerstone of industrial growth.

For Nigeria, this dynamic crop represents an economic asset of incredible potential. It also represents huge opportunities for rapid SME development as a means to economic diversification, poverty alleviation and employment generation. In 2008, the United Nations Organisation for Industrial Development (UNIDO) launched a $5 million programme to boost sustainable production of palm oil in Nigeria and Cameroon. Although relatively small in terms of initial outlay, the project aims to train farmers on more efficient methods of production and processing. Conservative estimates by UNIDO say at least a thousand news jobs will be created by the end of the four year project. Considering the extent of its resources and human capital, Nigeria stands to reap much larger economic benefits from an optimally-expanded palm oil industry. The palm oil industry is unquestionably vital to Nigeria's plans for accelerated growth and the establishment of a sustainable and closely interdependent economy. Reinvigorating the industry would contribute much to the entrepreneurial revolution that the country needs to turn its fortunes around.

Government intervention in this sector must be guided by a number of critical considerations:

- Maximising productivity in existing plantations so that scattered smallholdings can be converted into viable agricultural ecosystems.

- Minimising cost of production by developing high-yield varieties and improving efficiency in basic processing and refining activities.

- Creating effective backward and forward linkages for palm oil production and processing activities with focus on the larger domestic economy.

- Directing investment at marginal farmers and co-operatives that rely on wild groves or practice mixed farming on small plantations.

- Facilitating research and development, promoting public-private joint ventures and encouraging foreign investment with tax breaks and financial incentives.

- Revamping distribution and marketing networks to export-orientated standards; entering bilateral counter-trade agreements to avoid high tariffs and import restrictions.

- Ensuring compliance with international regulations on safety and quality of palm oil and processed products through wider use of technology.

- Implementing policies to address negative social development issues; for instance, promoting backward migration from urban areas to plantations.

Mining and the Entrepreneurial Revolution

In July 2009, the Nigerian Ministry of Solid Mineral Development (SMD) announced it had begun disbursing $10 million in grants to small scale miners and mining communities across the sub-Saharan nation. The federal government expressed hope the move would help the lowest tier of artisan and small-scale miners expand operations and jump to the middle or upper tier. More than anything, the announcement reiterated the government's renewed acknowledgement of the fact that mining communities are critical to achieving sustainable economic growth.

Revitalising the mining sector is part of extended government efforts to rectify massive imbalances in the economy, and the solid mineral sector is seen as crucial to overcoming the historic dependence on oil and gas. Nigeria boasts vast reserves of iron ore and coal, besides significant gold, uranium, gypsum, barite and tantalum deposits. Over the years, a sharp decline in the production of coal, tin and columbite weakened the mining sector and dragged its GDP contribution down to 0.5%.

Tin mining is one sector that has massive potential for expansion. Nigeria has reserves of the mineral in excess of 31,000 tonnes, most of it concentrated in the central Jos plateau, and was a major exporter before the oil boom of the 1970s. However, annual production fell drastically from 11,000 tonnes in 1975 to just about 2,000 tonnes currently. (Online Nigeria) Only a very small portion of the Jos deposits have so far been tapped; some estimates putting the total area of mining operation at just 4% of full potential. Official neglect of the sector has resulted in elaborate smuggling operations in unregulated mines. Further, over 80% of Nigeria's tin deposits occur at a depth of 36 metres below the ground, twice as deep as twenty years ago.

Although the mineral accounts for only a minor fraction of the country's foreign exchange, it appropriately indicates the gravity of obstacles facing the country's mining sector in general. Considering the fact that Nigerian tin is regarded as one of the top qualities in the world, there is scope for massive development of the sector. Stricter regulation and incentives for entrepreneurial ventures in tin mining can significantly boost export revenue, besides generating employment and sustaining extensive ancillary industries.

Since 1999, the government has rolled out significant incentives for existing and prospective investors in the mining sector. Fiscal adjustments include tax cuts, increase in capital allowances, and a three year tax holiday for new mining ventures. Additional tax exemptions were introduced to bolster exports and encourage further exploration and prospecting in solid minerals. The country saw the establishment of its first diamond cutting and polishing centre in 2002. In 2004, former President Olusegun Obasanjo successfully negotiated a $120 million World Bank assistance package to begin the Sustainable Management of Mineral Resources Project. The six-year long project which provides long-term, low-interest loans to the sector concludes in 2010 and has been the most serious attempt by far at sustainable management of Nigeria's mineral resources.

Along the same lines, former President Umaru Yar'Adua in pursuing a micro-grants programme for the mining sector, engaged commercial banks in providing seed funds and loans to small and medium-scale mining ventures. The Mines and Steel Development Minister stated that if the micro-grants are sustained, the sector would start contributing 20% of overall GDP within a span of ten years.

There are four essential challenges to Nigeria's mining aspirations, in general:

1) Increasing productivity in artisan and small-scale mining operations through socially and environmentally sound processes; diversifying the economy by empowering and consolidating scattered mining communities.

2) Developing public mining institutions that work efficiently in a transparent and modernised atmosphere, restructured to handle administrative loopholes and promote institutional capacity building through international best practices.

3) Facilitating better private and public sector co-operation to strengthen the mining infrastructure, and developing geological mapping and mineral assessment databases and information systems specifically designed to promote investment and exports.

4) Devising effective monitoring and assessment systems that can track multiple programmes simultaneously and propose necessary interventions, policy redirection's, and corrective measures in a comprehensive and timely manner.

Fishing and the Entrepreneurial Revolution

Nigeria's long history of fishing finds its most spectacular expression in the colourful Argungu festival, an event of international renown held annually in Kebbi state. After four days of cultural celebration, thousands of fisherman line up on the banks of the Matan Fada River for a competition. They descend into the muddy waters at the sound of a gunshot, with fish nets and gourds, in a bid to catch the biggest fish within an hour.

The image is a strikingly ironic symbol of the state of Nigerian fishing in general. The country enjoys more than 850 km of coastline, besides an enviable number of well-stocked rivers, inland lakes, lagoons and creeks. The topography, soil composition and rainfall patterns in this portion of sub-Saharan Africa support an abundance of aquatic life across freshwater, brackish, and saltwater ecosystems. However, Tilapia, Catfish, Carp and other freshwater species make up 80% of all cultivation in Nigeria, with commercial maritime trawling and deep-sea fishing remaining relatively under-exploited operations.

It is estimated that the fishing industry contributed approximately $60 million to the national economy in 2008, or roughly 4% of total agricultural output. (FAO) The sector currently accounts for 40% of the country's total animal protein intake and offers employment and livelihood to more than 3 million people, although its contribution to the economy is minimal.

Like mining, the fishing sector presents unique opportunities as both a poverty alleviation strategy and a tool for rapid entrepreneurial growth. Present levels of fish cultivation satisfy only a fraction of local requirement, with exports filling almost 95% of annual demand. Nigeria is in fact the top importer of fish on the African continent, sourcing more than 1.5 million tonnes of fish annually from international markets. Unofficial estimates suggest less than 10% of the country's fish farming potential is currently being utilised, with as much as 60,000 hectares of unused land available for expanding the sector. The fact remains that Nigeria's vast natural resources and human capital can be leveraged to promote extensive fishing as a means of ensuring not only exports but also food security.

Because of its extensive coastline and tropical climate, Nigeria has the potential to develop a diversified ecology for a range of commercially viable varieties of fish. The economic appeal behind fishing is tremendous, considering the secondary and tertiary enterprises it can generate. More efficient methods of inland cultivation and coastal trolling, executed in an export-oriented environment, can spur rapid growth of down-the-line industries. Fishing, by itself, has the potential of driving considerable enterprise development, transforming rural economies and generating direct and indirect employment opportunities in the process. The government's primary responsibility lies in providing opportunities for export of fish and fish products to international markets. Although viable data on the subject is lacking, the aggregate economic loss due to reduced local fish production is significant and needs focused policy initiatives to correct.

Early in 2008, the fishing industry in the coastal Nigerian state of Akwa Ibom was paralysed in a wave of extortion and boat capture unleashed by sea-borne pirates. The attacks forced trawlers to go on an indefinite strike, bringing the local economy to a standstill and causing terrible loss of revenue to the regional council. While this particular situation was eventually resolved, security remains just one of several major challenges restraining the expansion of Nigerian fishing. Other challenges include:

- The absence of a sustainable and progressive fisheries policy represents a fundamental hurdle, with lax government regulation routinely forcing small-scale operations out of business.

- Population expansion in coastal areas is giving rise to over-fishing and unscientific practices, destroying marine ecosystems and threatening underwater environments.

- Organised fishing attracts high capital expenditure in Nigeria as most of the necessary equipment, boats, feed, technology and know-how has to be imported.

- Infrastructure deficits severely hamper the storage, transport and marketing of fish in rural areas, making profitable urban markets unavailable to traditional fishing communities.

- Despite specific government efforts, commercial deep-sea fishing is out of reach for local entrepreneurs; the activity remains limited to the purview of foreign-owned companies.

Although the sector continues to receive sporadic government nudging and funding, the impact of these measures has been considerably restricted thus far due to lack of insight and effective implementation. Special schemes to promote fishing in target communities have also failed because of a low awareness about profitability in the business. Turning around this mindset could well prove to be one of the deciding challenges facing the Nigerian fishing industry.

The enterprise potential of this sector is doubly significant by the nature of the business. Fishing relies heavily on small and middle scale ancillary industries like canning, net-making and boat building, while supporting an additional base of activities in storage, processing and marketing. The net scope for employment generation, business development and poverty eradication through these allied activities make fishing deeply relevant to Nigeria's quest for inclusive economic growth.

Following are some of the most pressing arguments in favour of a rapid expansion of fishing activities:

- Aquaculture provides opportunities for optimal land use, allowing areas unsuitable for crops, to be developed into economically productive ponds and fisheries.

- Focused expansion of artisanal and small-scale fishing can help turn around rural economies rapidly by generating jobs and sparking entrepreneurial activity.

- In development-deprived areas and among rural communities, sustainable fish farming can help improve both nutritional and living standards.

- Nigeria's highly diversified tropical ecology makes fishing in brackish and fresh waters almost a zero opportunity-cost endeavour with infinite growth potential.

Industrialisation and the Entrepreneurial Revolution

In 2009, the United Nations Industrial Development Organisation (UNIDO) announced plans to conduct investor surveys in 22 African countries. A key goal of the survey in the case of Nigeria is to facilitate the creation of a Nigerian industrial master plan. The programme, which will also evaluate the impact of policy interventions on investors, is primarily aimed at bolstering government efforts to promote rapid SME development. UNIDIO officials in Nigeria claimed the survey would be of significant assistance to the private sector as well, helping expand operations and set performance benchmarks.

At the same time, the Manufacturers Association of Nigeria came out with a report identifying 37 companies that had closed down across the country over a space of just two weeks. The report once again confirms the bitter state of affairs of the Nigerian economy, where closures are a frequent and constant refrain. A complete account of contemporary Nigerian industry is in fact impossible without a mention of the de-industrialisation that continues to plague it. This is another core feature of the great 'Nigerian Paradox' of acute economic backwardness despite abundant natural and human resources.

The collapse of world oil markets in the early 1980s drastically reduced Nigeria's foreign exchange reserves and practically stalled economic growth. The cumulative effect of years of incoherent policies further upset the country's fragile international and domestic fiscal condition, causing massive inflation, unemployment and poverty. Nigeria's standing as a middle-income country was scuttled, and by the 1990s, it was confirmed as one of the poorest in the world. An even more demeaning fall in average living standards accompanied the loss of national fortunes.

The economic downslide proved especially harsh on the manufacturing sector, partly at least due to the over-dependence on oil exports that thwarted economic diversification. With local sourcing of raw material confined to all but a few industries, capacity utilisation plunged dramatically in import-dependent operations. Nigerian manufacturing is predominantly about isolated assembly-line functions with very limited or no backward connections to the economy. These and other factors combined to bring the total GDP contribution from manufacturing down from a little over 9% in 1981 to 6% by the end of the last century. (Ajayi)

Industrial decline has also, partly at least, been fed by unrealistic dependence on imports, often with shocking results. For instance, textile imports have shot up to a staggering N4.3 billion annually to keep up with burgeoning demand. Sadly, the number of textile industries in local operation fell from 140 in the 1970s to less than ten presently. More importantly, existing units operate at less than 50% capacity due to equipment and technical shortfalls. The over-dependence on imported goods, however, is by no means limited to textiles. Nigeria imports everything from machinery, chemicals, transport equipment, manufactured goods to live animals. Many in Nigeria consider it a shame that the government abandoned agriculture in favour of oil in the early 1980s. What is even more shameful is the fact that this formerly agrarian nation is now critically dependent on food imports. Nigeria imported $600 million worth of rice in 2008 alone, with local food production amounting to only a fraction of overall demand.

Nigeria's chronic dependence on imports is a result of many decades of misdirected policies that swamped local industry and wiped out diverse avenues of employment and wealth creation. Infrastructure deficits have been the largest hurdle to industrial expansion, and the country's

What Nigeria effectively needs are policies fostering rapid business development across sectors: In other words, an enterprise revolution that accelerates sustainable growth while simultaneously helping alleviate poverty and improve living standards. It also requires a radical rethink on the country's import policies, in a manner that focuses on improving productivity and employment through development of locally relevant enterprises. Import curbs can prove hugely beneficial for Nigeria, provided they are judiciously executed to promote industrial and small-business resurgence in prospective sectors. Agro-based industries related to processing and packaging comprise one area of massive growth potential, considering the country's vast stretches of arable land. Given its agrarian origins and tremendous human resource capital, the scope of employment in this sector is enormous and of significant consequence to long-term growth prospects for the Nigerian economy.

The complex socio-economic realities in this corner of West Africa often defy the best laid development plans, and it is no surprise that initiatives like the Nigerian Industrial Development Bank (established 1964) or the Structural Adjustment Programme of 1986 have consistently failed to deliver as far as improving Nigeria's industrial scenario goes. The severity of challenges facing it in this regard can hardly be overstated:

- Poor industrial performance and an unfavourable tax regime make the cost of manufacturing abnormally high, curtailing demand and reducing profitability.

- Most industrial activity is linked directly to foreign markets in terms of both inputs and delivery, with very few industries rooted in the local economy.

- Under-utilisation of resources - brought about by a plethora of causes including labour and security problems, falling demand and low liquidity – is a major industrial constraint.

- The infrastructure deficit, especially in power, is acute and a major impediment to viable industrialisation. Additionally, road and rail networks need massive overhaul.

- Trained manpower shortage in both technical and non-technical fields is a crucial shortcoming that affects productivity and optimisation in industrial operations.

- Low standards of education are deepening the already critical unemployment problem by turning out graduates who are unemployable in new or existing businesses.

- Socio-economic disparities and ethnic divides have provoked militancy and armed extremism to uncontrollable levels, especially in the oil-rich Niger Delta region.

- Official indifference, lax administration and ingrained corruption all combine to frustrate existing enterprises and deter the emergence of new ones.

Beyond just correcting these deficiencies however, Nigeria needs significant additional impetus to drive industrial development. In 2008, the government began pursuing a "cluster-concept" strategy to spur non-oil growth through the creation of industrial parks and special economic zones. Such clusters, often located near the coast or an international airport, offer lucrative investment options and tax breaks for new industries. The Nigerian Investment Promotion Commission, a single-window investment centre, is also actively involved in implementing policies and incentives that attract foreign industrial investors. The thrust of these initiatives has primarily been on encouraging public-private partnerships as a vehicle for rapid economic growth.

A central obstacle to industrialisation arises from the spatial distribution of existing plants and infrastructure. Industrial growth has been traditionally restricted to a few geographic locations, with virtually no inter-linking between locations and their respective industries. Widening the industrial distribution pattern remains a fundamental issue. One strategy for expanding the reach of industrial development is through production subcontracting. Industrial expansion is inseparably linked to rapid job creation, enterprise development and viable economic growth. Nigeria's goals would be well-nigh impossible to achieve without the active involvement of entrepreneurs in a regulated atmosphere of industrial networking and subcontracting.

Economic Diversification and the Entrepreneurial Revolution

The Nigerian economy is overwhelmingly dependent on oil, which accounts for 81% of government revenue and more than 97% of export earnings. Myopic policies pursued by successive military regimes in the final decades of the last century devastated the traditional agrarian economy and crippled growth in non-oil sectors. Consequently, Nigeria's growing oil wealth corresponded with a simultaneous decline of human development indicators and widening urban-rural divides. Massive imbalances in the economy spawned a thriving informal sector that continues to sustain most of Nigeria's 150 million people. The fundamental problem with the Nigerian economy is its failure to diversify. Instead of investing oil revenues in multi-sector economic growth or poverty alleviation, past governments frittered away national profits through unsustainable import reliance, poorly sustained policies, and corruption. The resulting fragility has been clearly evident during the global economic downturn which has impacted key areas of the Nigerian economy – from banking and foreign exchange reserves to the capital market and the mortgage sector.

Nigeria is better placed to develop a well-diversified economy than any other country in West Africa. The abundance of natural resources, mineral deposits and fertile land it enjoys is unrivalled, as is its substantial human resource pool. A range of initiatives devoted to promoting other sectors of the economy is already in place as part of the government's extensive reforms programme. The non-oil economy saw two-fold growth to 7% between 2001 and 2006, an encouraging sign in view of Nigeria's Vision 2020 goal of accelerated growth and economic consolidation. Optimising resource and raw material utilisation by developing a mass base of inter-linked enterprises is central to this scheme.

Given past experiences and present realities, Nigeria's resurgence is inseparably tied to business expansion in the small and medium sector. SMEs have proved reliable vehicles of economic transformation across the developing world because of the wide scope of their benefits – employment generation, foreign exchange conservation, optimal resource utilisation and equitable wealth distribution. The most convincing benefit of all, however, is the interdependence among businesses that SMEs foster – a critical consideration in the context of Nigeria's long term ambition.

Recent efforts by Abuja to promote a more inter-linked enterprise economy include:

- Reinforcing the financial sector with the 2004 bank consolidation programme to improve credit access to the private sector, specifically, small businesses.
- Privatising major public sector entities in oil production and marketing, construction, mining and ports to promote private participation and downstream enterprise development.

- Reduction of government expenditure and involvement in direct economic production through commercialisation, disinvestment and strategic mergers.

- Encouraging venture capital over debt by providing extensive tax relief and financial incentives to foreign private equity investors in key areas.

- Increasing focus on traditional activities like fishing, mining and agriculture that have considerable potential for entrepreneurial growth.

- Improving business skills and vocational training, most notably by making entrepreneurship education mandatory at the college level.

The Nigerian economy has not diversified as hoped. Even after a decade of multifarious reforms, more than half of all industrial raw material and consumer goods continue to be imported. Non-oil exports remain marginal while growth in potential boom sectors like tourism and textiles is sluggish. The dynamic economy running on rapid enterprise development that Nigeria is desperate for remains patently unachieved.

Some of the major hindrances to a more inter-linked entrepreneurial economy are:

- Low productivity in small-scale operations due to the wide prevalence of outdated technologies and business practices.

- Lack of socially relevant diversification models that optimise locally available resources and raw material.

- Predominance of stand-alone industries with little or no backward links to the local economy.

- The presence of a huge and thriving informal sector that operates outside the domain of government regulation.

- Massive infrastructure shortfalls in power and transportation that severely deter the evolution of small businesses.

- Rooted popular mindset against equity partnership and the overriding insistence on debt finance.

- Poverty, social unrest and violence that suffocate financial aspirations and blight market innovation.

The challenge of economic diversification is not limited to the developing world. Emerging and developed economies likewise are constantly seeking to reinvent and diversify their economic profile to reduce dependence on traditional sectors and take advantage of new opportunities in our globalised world. The oil-rich emirate of Saudi Arabia, which is well on the way to reinventing itself as a luxury tourist destination, is a striking example. Norway, one of the world's top crude producer, after Saudi Arabia and Russia, has likewise expanded its economy out of petrochemicals by establishing successful supply and service industries. These examples serve to bring out the heightened imperative for diversification that rests on oil-dependent economies, irrespective of their size.

Nigeria's oil reserves are estimated to run out before the end of 2030. Even if further reserves are explored over the coming years, the eventual decline of an oil-driven economy is inevitable. Nigeria's future standing on the world stage is, therefore, a *future beyond oil*. If this future is to be a prosperous one it will be because Nigeria has successfully realised a multi-faceted and interdependent enterprise economy based on a profound entrepreneurial revolution.

Sources

Ajayi, Dickson. Recent Trends and Patterns in Nigeria's Industrial Development *Africa Development,* Vol. XXXII, No. 2, 2007

Drucker, Peter F. *Innovation and Entrepreneurship*. New York: Harper Business, 1985.

Falola, Toyin and S.A. Olanreqaju, ed. *Transport Systems in Nigeria.* Maxwell School of Citizenship and Public Affairs, Syracuse University, Syracuse. 1986.

Fasua, K. O., Entrepreneurship Theory, Strategy and Practice. Abuja, Bee Printing &Publishing Co., 2006

Federal Government of Nigeria, "Obasanjo's Economic Direction: 1999 - 2003," Office of the Honorable Minister Economic Matters, Abuja, 2000

Hugo. K.; Masahiko, I.; & Masahiko, K. "Entrepreneurship in Emerging Economies: The Creation and Development of New Firms in Latin America and East Asia" Entrepreneurship. Inter-American Development Bank, 2002

Hopkins, G. A, An Economic History of West Africa. London: Longman, 1973

Lyakurwa, William M. "The Business of Exporting: Transaction Costs Facing Suppliers in Sub-Saharan Africa." Framework Paper presented at African Economic Research Consortium, April 23-4, 2007.
http://www.aercafrica.org/documents/export_supply_working_papers /Lyakurwa18DB3.pdf

Iwayemi, A., "Nigeria's Dual Energy Problems: Policy Issues and Challenges" International Association for Energy Economics Journal Fourth Quarter. 2008

King, D. T., "Transition period summary report" USAID / Nigeria Economic Growth Activities Assessment,. IBM Business Consulting Services, March, 2003

Lingelbach, David C., De La Vina, L., and Asel, P.,. "What's Distinctive about Growth-Oriented Entrepreneurship in Developing Countries?" UTSA College of Business Center for Global Entrepreneurship Working Paper No. 1 March 2005

National Planning Commission the National Economic Empowerment and DevelopmentStrategy (NEEDS), Abuja: National Planning Commission, 2004

Naude, W., (2010) "Promoting Entrepreneurship in Developing Countries: Policy Challenges" Policy Brief. United Nations University-World institute for Development Economics Research (UNU-WIDER). Number 4, 2010.

Organisation For Economic Co-Operation And Development, *OECD Observer.* Policy Brief, November 2006

Osalor, Peter "Poverty Eradication in Nigeria through Agriculture and Enterprise Revolution." *Vanguard.* http://www.vanguardngr.com/2010/07/19/poverty-eradication-in-nigeria-through-agriculture-and-enterprise-revolution-part-1/ accessed July 19, 2010.

Shokpeka, S. A.; and Nwaokocha, O. A. (2009) "British Colonial Economic Policy in Nigeria, the Example of Benin Province 1914 - 1954". Journal of Human Ecology. 28(1). pp 57-66

"The Enterpreneurship Challenge in Nigeria," knowledge.wharton.upenn.edu/article.cfm?articleid=1675 accessed March 10, 2008.

UNCTAD "Investment Policy Review: Nigeria" http://www.unctad.org/templates/webflyer.asp? docid=11325&intItemID=2068&lang, accessed August 9, 2010

UNFAO, "Fishery Country Profile, Federal Republic of Nigeria, March 2007," ftp://ftp.fao.org/FI/DOCUMENT/fcp/en/FI_CP_NG.pdf, accessed August 9, 2010

Usoro E.J,(1977) "Colonial Economic Development Planning in Nigeria, 1919-1939: An Appraisal." Nigerian Journal of Economic and Social Studies, 19: 121-136.

U.S. Department of State/Bureau of International Information Programs, "Principles of Entrepreneurship" 2007 http://www.ait.org.tw/infousa/zhtw/DOCS/enterp.pdf. accessed on 17th May, 2010

Van Buren, Linda "Nigeria: Economy," *Africa: South of the Sahara* 39th edit. London: Routledge, 2010.

World Bank Report, "Nigeria Policy Options for Growth and Stability", No. 26215-NGA, Washington DC: The World Bank, 2003.

World Trade Organization (2005), "Trade Policy Review of Nigeria", Geneva: World Trade Organization.

CHAPTER EIGHT

JOIN THE ENTREPRENEURIAL REVOLUTION TO ERADICATE POVERTY

"What lies behind us, and what lies before us are small matters compared to what lies within us."

- Ralph Waldo Emerson

"The distance is nothing; it is only the first step that is difficult. So take the step."

- Mme. Du Deffand

The Entrepreneurial Revolution and Poverty Alleviation

Beyond the individual, business enterprise is the answer for change in Nigeria and the whole of Africa. Entrepreneurship will reduce dependence on government funding as businesses will be able to provide products and services to their nations. Given an entrepreneurial mindset, even those in government will benefit from more efficient services. Further, more tax money will flow into the government, allowing for more opportunities to be created and programs implemented that will work on reducing the poverty rate. Businesses will also create jobs as they hire employees.

If Nigeria and other African and developing countries are to bring about an entrepreneurial revolution, they must know that it involves committed participants; resources; policy innovation and persistence; leadership; and publicity to win public support. The analysis presented in this book has made clear that if the majority of Africans who live in poverty are to be lifted out of this condition, governments and individuals must commit to the entrepreneurial revolution. As Obadina, a prominent political economist notes:

> African countries have stocks of raw entrepreneurial talent in small and medium scale enterprises which with training, technology and a supportive political environment, can evolve into capable managers and successful industrialists able to compete globally.

As President Kagame has declared, "entrepreneurship is the surest way" for Rwanda and Africa to develop. Our own experience convinces us that an entrepreneurial revolution is the only way forward for the African continent. Africa has the natural resources, the human resources, and the pressing need for this revolution. Your destiny as an individual, our destiny as a nation and the destiny of our continent is in our hands. Just as has been the case in China, India, Brazil and across Asia, and Latin America, a thoroughgoing entrepreneurial revolution is how we will bring millions of our people out of the cycle of poverty in Africa. Wishful and fuzzy thinking and relying on handouts will not get us there. If we are to achieve the entrepreneurial revolution, we must develop the mindset, and the enabling environment. We must move beyond an economy based largely on subsistence farming, subsistence enterprise, and the export of raw materials. We must grow and diversify the African economy, just like the Asian economy, and increasingly the economies of Latin America and Central Europe. We must shape a future where our economy is producing capital and consumer goods and providing services for our own markets and the global market. Just as the world sells the whole range of available goods and services to us, we must sell to the world. There is no other way if we are to alleviate poverty and realise our potential as individuals, nations and a continent. We must realise that we are our own liberators. We can seek assistance from other in terms of inspiration, models, and funds, but we must find our own way, and take control of our own destiny.

What will bring about and sustain the entrepreneurial revolution is individual passion and drive, and government support and facilitation of entrepreneurship. Individuals must envision and then pursue their entrepreneurial future. Governments must shape a conducive business environment in terms of infrastructure, the legal framework, financial assistance, and vocational and technical education. As individuals we must forget our fears of the risks associated with entrepreneurship. We must recognise that the biggest risks we take with our lives is actually taking a risk on ourselves, our future, our talents. As individuals we must get beyond our mindset of dependency. We will not got out of poverty by relying on handouts from charities or expecting the government to provide all. We must be self-motivated and self-actualised. We must turn our individual passions and visions into productive enterprises. We must get beyond our consumer mentality and develop the mindset of an entrepreneur, of a creator of goods and services.

For its part, government must be committed to the entrepreneurial revolution. Again, as Kagame argues:

> Government activities should focus on supporting entrepreneurship … to unlock people's minds, to allow innovation to take place, and to enable people to exercise their talents.

Government must encourage the development of the private sector. Enterprise start-up and growth must be supported. The private sector should be seen as more attractive than the public sector in terms of recognition and rewards. Making a successful living should be based on what you know, not whom you know. In addition to infra-structural development, small business loans, entrepreneurial training, etc. the government must also champion innovative entrepreneurs, publicise new opportunities, and encourage entrepreneurs to think outside the box of their immediate market and traditional goods and services. The 21st century economy is global and dynamic. Enterprise development must mirror this global economic reality.

The SMEs sector will be the basis of the entrepreneurial revolution. The recent global economic crisis has highlighted the failure of giant enterprises. Banks, insurance companies, airlines, car manufactures have all had to be bailed out by governments and have shed thousands of jobs. It is the SME sector that has proven to be the engine of economic growth and job creation. President Obama reminds us that "most new jobs [start] in small businesses, companies that begin when an entrepreneur takes a chance on a dream, or a worker decides it's time she became her own boss." The great business leaders are entrepreneurs; those individuals who have chosen to take control of their own destinies. Government must take heed, and followup on its voiced commitment to entrepreneurial development.

Putting in place a successful entrepreneurial revolution is, undoubtedly, a daunting task. "We have much more to do, and it will take time." (Kagame) But as another great revolutionary reminds us "A journey of a thousand miles begins with a single step." (Mao Zedong). We must take the first step, and then begin to lengthen our stride!

Joining The Entrepreneurial Revolution: A Practical Guide

The entrepreneurial revolution will be realised by the efforts of numerous individual entrepreneurs. As a conclusion to the book, we present a brief practical primer on enterprise start-up and growth. As we stated in chapter one, anybody can be an entrepreneur. And we have shown you the myriad of opportunities available in Africa to attract your entrepreneurial skills. This book has given you a head start on doing business in Africa. We have looked at the history of entrepreneurship, a case study of Nigeria, a profile of resources and opportunities available to build enterprises, policies that must be put in place and steps to form your own business. So what are you waiting for? There is no better time to start your own business than now.

Is a lack of education stopping you? There is no educational requirement for starting a business but you do need to know about the business you want to run. If you have a passion for clothes and want to run a designing firm, you need to know about fabrics, textures, prices, suppliers, consumers, etc.

Is a lack of money holding you back? There are many avenues to raise the money you need to start your business. You can save money by working for someone else first, borrow from relatives, or take a bank loan. Be creative when raising your start up capital: for example, you could start by selling popcorn to raise money to buy the equipment for your photography business.

Are you scared that corruption will kill your business? There are ways you can side-step corruption and even combat it. One of those ways is to do business or provide service to individuals and small businesses who will not demand or take bribes in order to buy your product or service.

Do you think you have the wrong location? Today, thanks to the internet, you can do business from virtually anywhere in the world. If you are planning to provide an information product or service, you need to have a web-site; in fact, every serious business today, needs a web-site in order to link with the world – both locally and internationally.

Whatever obstacles you believe will reduce your chances of being successful in your business, figure out ways around it. Don't let challenges stop you because there are so many benefits to owning your business. Advantages of entrepreneurship include:

Financial reward: You stand to earn more financially, provided you work hard and follow the rules, but you can only earn so much if you are working for someone else, no matter how hard you work.

Greater freedom: When you are your own boss, you can make decisions that are beneficial and productive, but you cannot exercise this kind of freedom when you work for someone else.

Job security: You cannot lose your job when you are working for yourself. No one can hold your salary or steal your pension. Your destiny is in the best of hands - your own.

Legacy benefits: Your business can be passed on to your children when you get tired of running it. But if you work for someone else, he is not going to pass your job to your child when you retire.

Fulfilment: Having a business that is not just successful but outlives you brings tons and tons of fulfilment, accomplishment, confidence, and recognition.

Ownership: When you own a business it gives you a better sense of ownership as you will be the one to dictate the pace of the business. You determine the hours and salaries both for you and your employees. You make all the decisions and take absolute responsibility.

You develop a higher spirit of innovation & enthusiasm:
Entrepreneurs, by nature, are enthusiastic and innovative. They see what could be done better; formulate ideas for better customer or client service, with higher visibility in addition to clear and targeted marketing. You must always focus on improving your business; in growing.

You live your passion: You have the opportunity to do what you are passionate about. So when you have a passion for something and you develop it into a business, you have succeeded in making your passion grow.

Financial freedom: By starting your own business, you enjoy financial freedom and will no longer have to depend on people for finances. You and you alone dictate the rhythm of your finances.

You have an opportunity to make great profit if your business is successful. *And once* your business is successful, you have various avenues to make more money. You can even expand your business to increase your income and profit.

A bright future: With diligence and a renewed drive to be successful, the future of the company and your future are sure to be great. ***You will be in complete Control of your destiny.*** You have a choice to either succeed or fail, and choosing any one of those will make or mar your destiny. So when you own your own business, you are in ultimate control of your destiny.

As defined earlier, the entrepreneurial revolution is a radical and co-ordinated attempt to accelerate wealth creation by promoting innovative businesses. It requires putting aside doubt, fear, and apathy to give entrepreneurship the attention it deserves in order to generate wealth that would pull nations out of poverty. It is this entrepreneurial spirit that is empowering countries like China, India, Russia, and others, to rise above poverty and under-employment.

As true of any successful revolution, no radical change happens overnight. No society can leapfrog from a stage of being a mere supplier of raw materials to one capable of orchestrating manufacturing and service feats. There are no short-cuts. However, a revolution is possible and absolutely necessary if Africa is going to climb out of poverty and under-employment.
To develop a nation of entrepreneurs, there must be a multi-sectoral, multi-level and multi-phase that breaks old modes of doing things.
Each individual, community, and nation must move decisively towards entrepreneurial thinking.

The top world economies – across Europe, the Americas and Asia – owe their prosperity in large part to the emergence of strong entrepreneurial movements that optimally leveraged available natural and human resource capital. Today, the same economies are once again banking heavily on enterprise development to bail them out of the present economic downturn. The entrepreneurs in these countries are creating new wealth and generating income-yielding opportunities for so many with their vision, daring, sense of innovation and passion for results. Even United States which has been the world's leading economic power for so long, the new creators of America wealth are the young entrepreneurs in the realm of information technology. There is a valuable lesson here that we should never miss. The most effective way to get closer to the threshold of prosperity and to be removed farther from the weight of poverty is through an entrepreneurial revolution. So how do you join the entrepreneurial revolution?

First, it is important to understand what a business is in order to avoid making mistakes that can hurt your chances of success. The term business is very broad and can be vague; for some it is any activity or trade with the sole aim of making profits. On the one hand, it can be said to be the occupation, work or trade in which a person is engaged in. On the other hand, a business can be defined as "an organisation that provides goods and services to people who want or need them". When many people think of business careers, they often think of jobs in large wealthy corporations, but for the entrepreneur, a business is any activity aimed at creating and keeping customers. There are basically two ways to carry out a business:

1) Sell goods (physical things like books, toys, cars, houses, information, etc).

2) Sell services (intangible things like nursery education, legal services, health care, insurance, etc.).

Many business-related careers exist in small businesses, non-profit organisations, government agencies, and educational settings. Conversely, your business may consist of selling both goods and services; for example if you are a computer dealer, you may sell goods (hardware and software) and services (maintenance, troubleshooting, and consulting). While it is very important to get a degree or some level of academic qualification, you can still go into business if you do not have one.

The future of our economy relies on you, the entrepreneurs. This is the dawn of a brighter and a brand new era of economic freedom. With the internet, YouTube and Twitter, we are about to enter the brightest era in economic history. Stop complaining about the rainstorms and learn to dance in the rain. Remove the fences in your mind, and flourish. Enter your passion; there is a market for anything of value, and that means there is a market for your passion. New markets are invented every day.

People will make money by doing what they love. Whatever stands in your way, find a way around it. There is no reason to fail. The most effective way to get closer to the threshold of prosperity and to be removed from the weight of poverty is through an entrepreneurial revolution. No government can control the destinies of entrepreneurs. No one else should determine your worth or value to society. I believe the more people decide to go after their dreams the faster the economy will get better. Creativity and success come from within. If you think you can, then you can.

How to join the Entrepreneurial Revolution

There are ten basic steps, as follows:

Step 1:
Have the right attitude. Becoming an entrepreneur is not an easy task but it gives you the ability to control your own destiny. There are many attitudes around and within you that will harm your entrepreneurial dream. Such attitudes include: blaming others for your situation, not taking responsibility for making progress in your own life, doing things anyhow or poorly, and begging others for your sustenance. As an entrepreneur, you must admit that your success is in your own hands – whether you progress or regress. Nobody is to blame, but you, and nobody will hand you 'contracts' or other resources on a platter. YOU HAVE TO MAKE SUCCESS HAPPEN. Expect that when you start your business, you will work hard, be focused, and be involved in every aspect of your business until you have reached a level of success when you can delegate to others.

Step 2:
Find your passion. Your choice of business must fit into your personality, passion, vision, strengths and other strong character traits. When your business matches your personality and passion, you have the energy and enthusiasm required to push your ideas through. For example, if you are passionate about children, you may decide to produce children's educational programs. You should not decide on your business idea based on what a friend has done or is doing; what everyone is flocking to; or what the latest trend is. Note that just because something works for another person doesn't necessarily mean it will work for you. Remember that entrepreneurship is individualistic and passion-driven. Every business starts with an idea, so it is important to have the right kind of idea; this is because the wrong idea can lead to the failure of a business. However, ideas alone do not make a business; you must research your idea.

Step 3:
Training and skills acquisition. After you have identified your passion, you must gain the necessary training to pursue your passion in the form of a profitable enterprise.

Step 4:
Carry out a Feasibility Study. Look around asking questions about your proposed business. How accessible are the raw materials you need? What will it take to produce your proposed goods or run your services? How much money could you expect to earn from your business in your first month, six months, or one year? Is there anyone who has been successful with this type of business? If so, what did they do to stand out? And how will you improve on the competition?

Step 5:
Write a Business Plan. A basic business plan should include the what, where, and how of your business idea. It should reflect your

mission for your enterprise, goals, personal skills, needs, available resources, level of risk, and the nature of your business. One of the most important aspects of starting your own business is that it gives you an opportunity to do what you enjoy. As stated in Step 1 above, you should follow your passion or promote your talents when considering your enterprise. Also consider the types of products and services needed in your community.

Preceding chapters have given you insight into goods, services, and sectors of the Nigerian and African economies that can provide you with business opportunities. Indeed, the field is wide-open. Further, your business should detail what resources you will need to make your business successful. Will you need cement, access to running water, or immediate hiring of several employees? In your plan, lay out what your upfront costs would be to make your business a reality. Your business plan does not require hundreds of pages or charts, you simply need to put on paper (to keep you on track), what your business goals are, how you will fund them, and what you will bring in.

What? - What is your idea? What are its components? What is its value? What could you do with your idea to develop it into a thriving business? What are you trying to achieve by running this business?

Where? - Where would by business be located? Do you need to purchase office space right away or could you run my business from my home? How do you reach customers with your product or service wherever they are? Many people can only reach local markets but you can plan a wider reach by having a web-site and networking internationally.

How? – How do you bring your idea from your head to the marketplace? How do you find money to start your business? How do you tap into available resources and find accessible ones? How will you run your business? How will you deal with risks and challenges that arise from running the business?

Step 6:
Write a Marketing Plan. An initial marketing plan helps you to focus on your potential customers. You should interact with them, know what they like about your products/services, know how much they are willing to pay, and when they are most likely to buy. Will you market your product/service by word-of-mouth, radio, television, or internet advertisement, or would you sell through an established network? When you have a clear marketing plan, you are able to do the thing most critical to your business – SELL.

Step 7:
Obtain Funding. Your business plan should reveal how much you need to start your business. Now, you need to find the money to start. There are a number of ways and places you can find the money you need. These include: family member loans/gifts, Susu contribution, a small business loan from a bank, or investment capital from angel investors. Your best bet is to start small, thereby limiting the amount of capital you need. After you have started small, you can always invest your profits back into the business to grow it.

Step 8:
Build your Infrastructure. This does not mean you should build a factory to begin to manufacture your products. It means you should put in place the support beams of your business – bookkeeping, web-site, customer records – key elements that tell you whether you are making a profit or not. You must always be able to track the progress of your business. You should be able to answer questions such as: how much money did you make last week, last month, and even last year? How much did you spend in the same time period? How many customers do you have? Where do you do business best?

Without adequate infrastructure, you would only guess at whether you are moving forward or backward.

Step 9:
Plan for Contingencies (unexpected emergencies). Brace up for the challenges ahead because you will encounter obstacles. Having a plan in place when the challenges come helps you to get through with limited damage to your business. For example, if you live in Nigeria and must use electricity to run your business; have you bought a generator to combat power outages? What do you plan to do about the security of your business? What if you need to take a break, who will run your business? Making plans to combat challenges does not imply you are asking these challenges to come your way; it simply ensures that you don't fall apart at the merest hint of an obstacle.

Step 10:
Step out Confidently. The noted economist Jean-Baptiste Say in 1803, as cited by Hisrich and Peters (2002), defined an entrepreneur as someone who consciously moves economic resources from area of low yield to area of high yield. He redeploys people, material, money and co-ordinates the processes necessary for efficient large scale industrial/trade development. As an entrepreneur, step out confidently; if you don't have confidence in your own product or service, no one else will. Don't be hesitant or tentative. And don't make excuses for your product or service before your user uses it; simply sell what you have to sell.

Seize the Moment

The world is your oyster, and opportunities abound. The global economy is constantly reinventing itself with new technologies, new products, new demands, and new ways of delivering goods and services. New and emerging occupations that did not exist at the beginning of the century are providing enterprise development opportunities and millions of jobs in the United States, China, India, Brazil, and across the globe. Such opportunities to pursue enterprise development also abound in Nigeria. They include:

- Outsourced and privatised government services: IT based delivery of government services, to provide 21st century "smart" administration for cities.

- ICT training and applications: Web site development, call centres, e-marketing, E-learning (online teaching/training)

- Solar power applications.

- Entrepreneurial training and workforce development training.

- Private security services.

- Environmental sanitation.

- Natural skincare, hair grooming and homeopathic products, herbal (rural based industries) products.

- Afro-centric furnishings and fashions.

- New niche markets of the 21st century – green products and packaging, organic products, fair traded products, overseas and diaspora communities.

- Tourism development: eco-tourism, cultural and Pan-African tourism, world heritage and history tourism and related hospitality industry infrastructure and services

***SEIZE THE MOMENT AND JOIN THE ENTREPRENEURIAL
REVOLUTION.***

In conclusion it is never too late to become what you can and should become. Just do it by taking the next step today. And when you stand before God, at the end of your life, you can boldly say 'I used every talent and gift You gave me'.

To God be the glory!

Nigerian Entrepreneurs

Register now @
www.nigerian-entrepreneur.com

FOR FREE

African Entrepreneurs
www.theafricanentrepreneurs.com
REGISTER NOW FOR
▸ Free tax information
▸ Tips on entrepreneurship
▸ Free newsletter
▸ Investments in Africa
▸ Business promotion
Meet other entrepreneurs from Africa.
Business networking, discussion forums,
contacts, advertisements and investments.
www.theafricanentrepreneurs.com

<u>**RESOURCES**</u>

Thank you for your Investment in 'Entrepreneurial Revolution: *Solution for Poverty Eradication'*.

The following books are out now
-Why and How to Start your Own Business: *A Simple Guide for Business Start-ups*
-*How to Identify and Fund your Business: 200 Business Ideas and 28 Ways to Raise Capital for Your Business*
-How to Prepare a Business Plan: *A Step by Step Guide*
-Success in your Business: *How to Become a successful Entrepreneur*

For Entrepreneurial Workshops and Seminars contact: www.peterosalor.com

To Order Online HYPERLINK
"http://www.peterosalor.com/"http://www.peterosalor.com

Recommended Resources

Tax Advice and Consultancy, UK
Peter Osalor and Co.
 HYPERLINK "http://www.posagconsulting.com/"http://www.posagconsulting.com

Marketing Your Company

Web hosting
Hostgator HYPERLINK "http://secure.hostgator.com/~affiliat/cgi-bin/affiliates/clickthru.cgi?id=osalorp" \n
_blankhttp://secure.hostgator.com/~affiliat/cgi-bin/affiliates/clickthru.cgi?id=osalorp

Domain Registration & Hosting
1and 1 HYPERLINK "http://1and1.co.uk/?affiliate_id=237255" \n
_blankhttp://1and1.co.uk/?affiliate_id=237255

E-Mail Marketing Software
Aweber HYPERLINK "http://www.aweber.com/?357303" \n
_blankhttp://www.aweber.com/?357303

Get Response HYPERLINK
"http://www.getresponse.com/index/posalor"http://www.getresponse.com/index/posa
lor

Web Design and Marketing Company
London Top Web Design – London, UK

HYPERLINK
"http://www.webdesign.londontop.co.uk/"http://www.webdesign.londontop.co.uk
Internet Marketing and Coaching
New Dawn Concepts, London, UK
HYPERLINK http://www.adedalmeida.com/

Other Books By Peter Osalor

Purchase all the books within the Entrepreneurial Development Series.
They are available online and in bookstores near you.

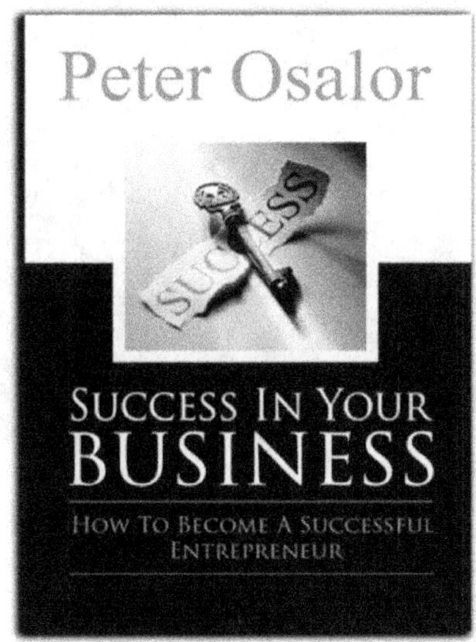

Peter Osalor

ECONOMIC
TRANSFORMATION

*From a Poor Person to a Wealthy Person,
From a Poor Nation to a Wealthy Nation*

Entrepreneur, Entrepreneurship, Entrepreneulism,
MSME, Entrepreneurial Revolution

COMING SOON!

YOUTH
EMPOWERMENT
AND
ENTREPRENEURIAL
REVOLUTION
A Solution for Youth Restiveness,
Job Creation and a Prosperous Society
Peter Osalor

COMING SOON!

Women
Empowerment
& Entrepreneurial
Revolution
The solution for a prosperous society, poverty
eradication and wealth creation
Peter Osalor

COMING SOON!

www.ingramcontent.com/pod-product-compliance
Lightning Source LLC
Chambersburg PA
CBHW051053050726
47592CB00002B/509